The Book of Love

Brief Meditations

Richard Clements

En Route Books and Media, LLC

Saint Louis, MO

⊕*ENROUTE*
Make the time

En Route Books and Media, LLC
5705 Rhodes Avenue
St. Louis, MO 63109

Cover credit: Sophia Clements

ISBN-13: 979-8-88870-019-8
Library of Congress Control Number: 2022951967

In loving memory of my parents,
Mary Anne and Pat Clements

Measure thy life by loss
and not by gain,
Not by the wine drunk, but
by the wine poured forth,
For love's strength standeth in
love's sacrifice,
And he who suffers most has most to give.
I am now ready to be offered.

Lilias Trotter

Acknowledgments

In writing this book, I have relied heavily upon the theology of Hans Urs von Balthasar, the brilliant Roman Catholic theologian from Switzerland. I have also drawn significant inspiration from the thought of Josef Pieper, Saint Thomas Aquinas, Pope Saint John Paul II, Pope Emeritus Benedict XVI, and C. S. Lewis.

TABLE OF CONTENTS

PART III THE TWO MOVEMENTS OF LOVE

PART IV THE VIRTUE OF SELFLESSNESS

PART V THE MANY FACES OF LOVE

PART VI THE FULFILLMENT OF ALL DESIRE

PART VII BEING SOMEBODY, GOING SOMEWHERE

INTRODUCTION

It's All about Love

"Love is everything…."
Saint Thérèse of Lisieux

"Love is the whole and more than all"
E. E. Cummings

Why did I write *The Book of Love*? Well, the most important reason was so that whenever I hear the pop song "(Who Wrote) The Book of Love?"[1], I could say, "I did!"

Oh yeah, there were a couple of other reasons too: something about love being the ultimate reality, and something about our ultimate destiny hinging on our choice of whether to say Yes or No to love….

But seriously: it turns out that love is what life is all about. Love is the answer to the big questions in life that we all wonder about sooner or later:

➢ Why is there something rather than nothing? *For the sake of love*

➢ Why are we all here? *To share forever in the divine life of God, which is an eternal circulation of love*

➢ Why am I, in particular, here? *To carry out a mission of love that is unique to me and share forever in the eternal circulation of love*

➢ Is there any ultimate meaning or purpose to life? *Yes, and they are found in love*

➢ How can we attain ultimate happiness? *Through love*

➢ How can we attain ultimate freedom? *Through love*

➢ How can we attain ultimate peace? *Through love*

Yes, it turns out that life is all about love. Not wealth, not pleasure, not status, not power, not knowledge, but love. All of those other things can be good, even very good. But they're not the *ultimate* good.

Life is a school of love. We're all here to learn how to love. We all have our origin in Love, and our intended destination is Love. We are all *homo viator*: people on the way; travelers; wayfarers; voyagers; adventurers. The problem is, many of us have forgotten what our destination is, or even that we have a destination at all.[2] We are all on a journey *ad Amorem*, a journey to Love. Whether we arrive there or not and the condition in which we arrive depend on the extent to which we open or close our hearts and minds to love.

The *real* Book of Love *was* written by "someone from above". There *is* an "absolute being" (i.e., God), and the essence of that absolute being is *love*. God did not need the world in order to be God, nor did God need the world in order to be love, but God, purely out of divine love and freedom, chose to create the entire cosmos so that all of creation (including us human beings) could share in the divine life and love of God. In Jesus Christ, God reveals to us that his essence, and therefore the essence of being itself, the essence of *life* itself, is *self-giving love*. To give oneself away in self-sacrificial love is to be truly alive. The divine life consists precisely in an eternal circulation of self-giving love among the Father, Son, and Holy Spirit. We were created to share forever in that dynamic flow of love. We were created to dwell eternally in the divine life and love of God, and to pass that life and love on to others. *That's* why we're here. As Hans Urs von Balthasar, the brilliant Roman Catholic theologian from Switzerland, so aptly expressed it, "The meaning of the world is love."[3]

However, because love is genuine only if it is freely given and freely received, God gives us the freedom to choose whether to open our hearts and minds to love. Life is a grand drama in which our ultimate destiny, as well as the fulfillment of our deepest desires, hinges on our decision of whether to say Yes or No to love. We can choose to remain imprisoned within the cramped confines of our self-centered, self-enclosed egos, or we can break out of our finitude and into the "immeasurable spaces of freedom"[4], into the divine life of God, which is an eternal circulation of love.

PART I

THE SCHOOL OF LOVE

1.

The School of Love

We're all here to learn how to love. Life is a school of love. The things that happen to you in life are meant to help you learn how to love. The people who cross your path in life are meant to help you learn how to love, and you're meant to help them learn how to love, too.

We're all on a journey back to God, a journey *ad Deum*. It's just that some of us don't realize that yet, or have forgotten it, or else don't want to believe it. But we are. We all came from God, and we're all intended to return to God. Only in God will we find the ultimate happiness, freedom, purpose, and peace that we so desperately desire.

The little three-word phrase "God is love" (1 John 4:16) is the most profound statement ever uttered by a human being. For some people, however, the phrase "God is love" has become so familiar as to have become almost trite. They may acknowledge that it is true in the abstract, but it is not a truth that they allow to impact their daily lives in any significant way: "'God is love' sounds nice, but it doesn't pay the bills" – this seems to be the attitude of some people. Other people reject the claim that "God is love" entirely.

Many of us need to consider (or reconsider) the profound meaning and implications of the claim that "God is love". This little phrase not only claims that God exists; it also makes a startling claim about what God *is*. The claim is not just that God *has* love, but rather that God *is* love. Love is what God *is*. God's *essence*, the core of who and what God is, is *love*. Not thought, or power, or freedom, or knowledge, or any of the other things that we human beings might have expected or predicted to be the essence of God, but *love*.

But "God is love" is not just a statement about God. It's also a statement about the nature of existence, the nature of life itself. God is not just one more being among many. God is not some "super-being" with superhuman powers. Some atheists seem to derive pleasure from attacking such images of God, but that's not the God in whom we Christians believe. No, God is not just one more being among many; God is *Being itself* (Exodus 3:14; John 8:58). God is the Mind behind all that exists, the Mind that gave rise to all that exists and that sustains everything in existence from moment to moment, the Source and Ground of all that exists, the uncaused Cause of all that exists. So if God is Being itself, and the essence of God is love, then *the essence of Being itself is love*. Love is what Being *is,* so love is what *being* is meant to be. To love is to be, and to love more fully is to *be* more fully. The more fully we join in the dynamic of love, the more fully we share in Being, and the more fully *alive* we are.

Some of the ancients described human life as a process of *exitus* and *reditus*: a *going out* from God when we are born into this life so that we might then freely choose whether or not we want to *return* to God forever. Our life is intended to be a journey back to

God, a journey back to Love. We were born for love. We were made from and for love. We were created to dwell forever in the divine Love, but whether we end up there or not depends on whether we accept God's offer of a share in the divine life.

Life is a beautiful and profound and mysterious drama in which our ultimate destiny, our *eternal* destiny, hinges on our choice of whether to say Yes or No to Love and to love. The stakes couldn't be higher. So why does God leave the choice up to us? Again, it's because love, to be genuine, has to be both freely offered and freely accepted. God doesn't work by force, but rather by *persuasion*. God freely offers us the gift of a share in the divine life and love, but it's up to each of us to choose whether to accept the gift or not. We're all enrolled in the school of love, but it's up to each of us whether we make the most of the opportunity or choose to drop out.

2.

The Eternal Circulation of Love

The divine life of God is an eternal circulation of love among the Father, Son, and Holy Spirit. You and I and every other human being who has ever existed were created to share forever in that eternal flow of love. You and I and every other human being were meant to be united forever with God and with all of our fellow human beings who choose to accept God's offer of a share in the divine life. Only there, only within that eternal circulation of love, will our hearts find the happiness, freedom, purpose, and peace that they so desperately desire. But to be able to share as fully as possible in the divine life and love, we have to learn how to love as God loves.

At the heart of the divine love, at the heart of the divine life, lies the *gift of self*. The essence of love is the gift of self, because the essence of *Love* is the gift of self. God *is* self-gift. Giving is not just something that God *does*; giving is what God *is*. The divine life of God is an eternal exchange of the gift of self among God the Father, God the Son (Jesus Christ), and God the Holy Spirit. From all eternity, God the Father pours out the gift of himself in begetting God the Son. The Father selflessly shares his total divinity with the Son, giving the Son everything he is except his status as Father, his status as the "unoriginate Origin"[5], which he cannot give away. The Son eternally receives the Father's gift of self in love and gratitude, selflessly giving the Father the gift of himself in return. This reciprocal self-gift of Father and Son is so perfect, so complete, that it "spirates" a third divine Person, the Holy Spirit, who is the Spirit of love flowing between Father and Son. The Holy Spirit joins with the Father and the Son in the eternal exchange of the gift of self that constitutes the divine life. In God, we see the true nature of love revealed: *Love is the selfless gift of self, given and received.* The divine bliss consists precisely in this eternal circulation of love among the Father, Son, and Holy Spirit.[6]

We were born to share forever in the eternal circulation of love that is the divine life. But to participate as fully as possible in the divine life, we have to learn to selflessly give and receive the gift of self in love. That's what we're here to learn how to do. And the more fully we learn to do that, the more fully we can share in the divine love and life and bliss.

3.

Blood Circulating in the Body of the Cosmic Christ

But how could we humans possibly share in the divine life of God? How could we, who are finite beings, be united with the infinite God? There is an infinite chasm between us finite human beings and God. We cannot leap over the abyss separating the finite from the infinite. We need a lifeline of some kind to be thrown across to us from the shores of infinity, a bridge of some sort that will span the abyss and enable us to cross over into the divine realm. Jesus Christ is that lifeline; Jesus Christ is that "vaulting bridge"[7] who spans the abyss separating us finite beings from the infinite God. Jesus has forever united the human with the divine in himself, thereby making space for all human beings (indeed, the entire cosmos!) within the divine life of God.

Think about it: God and humanity, the infinite and the finite, united in the one person of Jesus Christ, in such a way that the path for us to transcend our finitude and participate in the infinity of Being, to share in the divine life of God forever, has been opened up to all human beings and to the entire cosmos. Seemingly impossible; seemingly incredible. But if it is true (which it is), then this one person would be the answer to the riddle of human existence. That is why our individual destinies are determined by our answer to the single most important question confronting us in life: Yes or No to Jesus Christ, which is a Yes or No

to love and therefore a Yes or No to God and to our ultimate fulfillment as human beings. We were all born to be "blood circulating in the Body of the cosmic Christ", in Balthasar's beautiful
phrase.[8] By uniting ourselves to the Body of Christ, we are united
with God and with all the other members of that Body. By uniting
ourselves to the Body of Christ, we join in the eternal circulation
of love that is the divine life and find therein our ultimate fulfillment.

4.

Mission: Implausible

But God did not intend for us to be merely passive members of the Body of Christ. God has entrusted to each of us a unique role, a unique *mission of love*, within the Body of Christ. That may seem hard to believe at first: God has given *me* a special mission of love to carry out in life? But it's true. Each of us is given the great privilege, and the solemn responsibility, of helping to pass on the divine love to other members (and prospective members) of the Body of Christ. Which includes everyone, because God wants everyone to share in his divine life and love forever (Matt 18:14; 1 Tim 2:4). You have been given a unique mission to share the divine love with others. The unique meaning and purpose of your life lies in your mission of love. Your mission is irreplaceable. No one else can fulfill your mission for you. No one else's life will touch the exact combination of people that your life will touch. No one else can add to the eternal circulation of love the contribution that you were born to make. What is the mission of love with which God has entrusted you?

5.

Red Blood Cell or Glob of Plaque?

For most of us, the mission of love that God has in mind isn't some dramatic, world-changing mission, something that will have a huge impact on the world as a whole or draw a lot of attention to us. Instead, most of us are called to *local* missions of love. There's a saying that goes something like "Strive to make your little corner of the world a better place." It's a good saying. If we *all* did that, the whole *world* would be a much better place.

The absolutely best way to make your "little corner" of the world a better place is to spread some of the divine love to that little corner. Start at home. How can you be more loving to your spouse? How can you be more loving to your children? Then extend yourself further: how could you be more loving to your friends? Your neighbors? Your co-workers? The people you perceive to be your "enemies"?

We all have a choice in life: we can be red blood cells flowing within the Body of Christ, helping to carry life-giving oxygen (the divine love) to other members and prospective members of that Body, or we can choose to be globs of plaque, clogging the arteries of that Body and obstructing the flow of divine love. Most of us are a little bit of both. Resolve to be more of a red blood cell and less of a glob of plaque.

PART II

THE GIFT OF SELF

6.

The Greatest Gift

The gift of self: if you're married, that's what your spouse wants from you: your spouse wants *you*; your *self*; your *heart*. Ideally, your spouse reciprocates your gift of self with his or her own gift of self to you. If that's not where your relationship is at right now, make a change. No, don't change spouses. Change the way you're *treating* your spouse, and watch how those changes can improve and strengthen your marriage. Make a genuine effort to be more giving, more generous, more sacrificial, for your spouse's sake. Hopefully, sooner or later (hang in there if it takes a while), they'll notice the change in you, and they'll become more willing to reciprocate with their own sacrificial gift of self. *Be the change* you want to see in your marriage instead of just wishing for a better relationship, and you can help bring about that change.

The gift of self: if you have children, that's what your children want from you, too: *you*; your *self*; your *heart*. Of course, your children want and need many other things from you: food, clothing, shelter, education, etc. But what your children most need from you is...*you*. That's why it's so important that you spend as much time as possible with your kids while they're growing up. It's a cliché, but it's true: you never get the years of their childhood back, so make the most of them while you can. Your kids need as much of your time and attention as you can give them. They want to get to know you (at least until they're teenagers, when they may think they have you all figured out already anyway), and they want you to get to know them. When your young child excitedly asks you to look at the picture he or she just drew, they're not just looking to share a picture; they're trying to share *themselves* – their talents, their interests, etc. They're not looking for just a nod and a perfunctory "That's nice". Yes, they're looking for your affirmation and your approval (more about that later), but they're also looking to *connect* with you. They want you to take a genuine interest in their work, and thereby, an interest in *them*. Put the cell phone down and really *look* at the drawing (and at your child!) Give them the chance to talk about what they drew, why they drew it, etc., because that gives them the chance to tell you about themselves, to share themselves with you. It's one of the ways they're trying to tell you they love you. By giving them your undivided attention and by taking a real interest in the picture they're trying to share with you, you're not only opening yourself up to receive the gift of self your child is offering you; you're also giving them the gift of your own self in return.

The gift of self: if you're a human being, that's what *God* wants from you. God wants *you*; your *self*; your *heart*. And God doesn't ask for anything that he hasn't already given. Jesus Christ is God's self-gift to the world. God wants to be united with each of us forever. We were created for union, union with God and our fellow human beings. The Son of God became one of us to make that union possible. Jesus is God's gift of his heart to the world, the gift of his heart to each and every one of us. And God's hope is that we will respond to his gift of self with our own gift of self in return.

7.

Hand It Over

To give the gift of self to God in love is to entrust our lives to God, to hand our lives over to God. Unfortunately, many of us find this to be rather difficult to do. If God has given us the gift of himself, the gift of his heart, in Jesus Christ, why are we so reluctant to respond with our own gift of self in return? There can, of course, be many reasons, but one of the main reasons is *control*. We want to be in control of our lives. But to give the gift of self in love requires that we give up some of that control. In fact, we have to be willing to *surrender* ourselves to the beloved.

Admittedly, the concept of "surrender" often carries with it some negative connotations – connotations like defeat, failure, weakness, etc. But nothing could be further from the truth when it comes to "surrender" in the context of love. Loving self-surrender is a sign of *strength*, not weakness. Loving self-surrender is actually the ultimate exercise of one's power over one's own life. Which requires more strength: to cling to one's ego throughout a life lived in the self-centered pursuit of pleasure, power, status, etc., or to give one's self away in love? As André Gide once observed, "Complete possession is proved only by giving. All you are unable to give possesses you."[9] To cling to one's self is to be enslaved to the self, to be at the mercy of the self's whims and desires, to be imprisoned within the walls of one's ego. In contrast, to give one's self away in love is, paradoxically, to be in full possession of one's self, breaking out of the dungeon of the ego and into the infinite spaces of the divine love.

Still, the prospect of giving oneself away in love to another, even to God (and for some of us, *especially* to God), can be frightening for many of us. What would God do with my heart? What would God demand of me? What would my life be like if I handed myself over to God?

Well, in a word...*better.* Surrendering your heart to God makes your life better because surrendering your heart to God aligns you with the purpose for which you were made. You were made for union with God and your fellow human beings. You were made to share in the divine life of love forever. But to be able to flow within the Body of Christ, you have to be willing to let go of some control over your life. You have to be willing to let go and love. You have to be willing to hand your life over to God.

8.

Giving Back to the Giver

We tend to think of our lives as entirely our own, to do with completely as we please, but they're not. Our lives are a total gift from God, given to us out of God's love for us, out of God's desire to share his life with us. "Already to exist is a work of love!"[10] The fact that you're here, that you're alive, is, in itself, a sign of God's love for you. You didn't *have* to exist; innumerable others could have existed in your place. But God chose *you*. God chose to give *you* the gift of life, to offer *you* a share in the divine life. God chose you for a unique place within the Body of Christ. God chose you for a unique mission of love within the Body of Christ, a mission that no one else can fulfill.

Surrendering your life to God is then, in reality, merely offering back to God, in gratitude, the gift that you have already been given. Surrendering your life to God is an acknowledgment of that gift, and an offer to allow God to use your life in whatever way God wills for the good of the rest of the Body of Christ. To surrender your life to God is to offer yourself as a channel, a conduit, for the divine love.

Surrendering your life and your heart to God can begin right now, today, with a simple prayer. Maybe something like the following, or something similar expressed in your own words:

Thank you, Lord, for the gift of my life. I give my life back to you in love and gratitude for that gift. Do with my life as you will. Use me as your instrument in the world. Help me to see and fulfill the mission of love you have planned for me.

Learning to *completely* surrender our lives and our hearts to God is actually a lifelong process. We may sometimes feel the gravitational pull of our egos, seeking to draw us back into our old self-centered ways, away from God and our mission of love. That's why it's good to pray some version of this prayer of surrender on a regular basis: as a repeated expression of our love for God, as an ongoing request for God's guidance and grace, and as a reminder to ourselves of the commitment that we have made to God and to our God-given mission.

9.

Plug In

Surrendering your life to God doesn't make you weaker; it makes you *stronger*. Surrendering your life to God brings a special kind of strength: the strength to be more loving to other people. It becomes easier to hand yourself over in love to other people when you've already handed yourself over to God. Opening up your heart and mind to God inserts you more deeply into the eternal circulation of love, enabling the divine love to flow more freely through you to the other people in your life. You've plugged into the power Source. When you've handed your heart over to God and to your God-given mission of love, God will supply you with the love and the energy to carry out that mission. Which is a really good thing, because you'll need it. The path of self-giving love is a demanding path. It's the path of the cross. But it's also the path to the Resurrection. The only path.

10.

Love Is Life that Pours Itself Forth[11]

Why must the path of self-giving love also be the path of the cross? Can't we be loving people without having to travel the way of the cross? No, we can't. At least, we can't be the *deeply* loving people that God has called us to be (Mt 16:24; Mk 8:34; Lk 9:23). Because we were created to share in the divine love, we're called to learn to love as *God* loves. And that means being willing to *break ourselves open and pour ourselves out* in love for God and our fellow human beings, just as Jesus did on the cross. And that requires busting some holes in the walls that we have all built around our egos, the walls that get in the way of love: walls of pride, and self-protection, and self-pity, and fear, and prejudice, and hatred, and anger, and…the list goes on and on.

Sacrifices made for the sake of the beloved and suffering undergone for the sake of the beloved help to punch holes in those walls we've built around our egos, holes that allow the divine love to flow into us more freely and to then flow back out of us to God and neighbor. Self-sacrifice and suffering for the sake of others help us break out of the self-imposed dungeons of our egos and join more fully in the eternal circulation of love. That's why sacrifice and suffering turn out to be required courses in the school of love. That's why we all have to be willing to walk the way of the cross. Yes, it can be painful (sometimes, very painful) to open ourselves up to love, to open ourselves up to self-sacrifice and suffering for the sake of love. But doing so also turns out to be immensely fulfilling, even joyful. We are most fully alive when we are most fully breaking ourselves open and pouring ourselves out in loving self-gift to God and neighbor, for it is precisely then that we participate most fully in the superabundant, overflowing love and life of God.

11.

Food for the Journey

In the sacrament of the Eucharist, Jesus provides us with the strength and sustenance we need to tread the path of the cross, to make our way through the school of love that is this life. In the Eucharist, Jesus breaks open his Body and pours out his Blood as literal food and drink for us so that we can become more fully incorporated into his Body, more fully united with God in love. But he also breaks open his Body and pours out his Blood for us in order to strengthen and fortify us with the divine life and love, so that we can, in turn, break ourselves open and pour ourselves out in love for others. That is why the Eucharist has sometimes been referred to as "food for the journey". The Eucharist nourishes and supports us on our own journey toward Love, and the Eucharist also strengthens us to go out and become "food for the journey" for other people.

A couple of years before he died, Pope Saint John Paul II wrote an encyclical in which he encouraged Catholics to rediscover their sense of amazement at the Eucharist.[12] It's a message that many of us need to hear today, especially at a time when surveys indicate that only 31% of Catholics believe in the Real Presence of Jesus in the Eucharist[13], and only 39% of Catholics attend Mass on a weekly basis.[14] Here are three ways to regain or strengthen your sense of amazement at the Eucharist: 1) Read, and re-read, and meditate upon, the words of Jesus regarding the Eucharist in the sixth chapter of the Gospel of John. Jesus makes it abundantly clear that the Eucharist is his *actual* Body and Blood and not merely some "symbol" of his love for us. Jesus also emphasizes the absolute necessity that anyone who claims to be his follower allow himself to be fed by the Eucharist; 2) If you're not already attending Mass every week, start doing so. Jesus can't feed you with the Eucharist if you don't show up at the table. You wouldn't choose to starve yourself physically; don't starve yourself spiritually, either. Commune with the heart and mind of Jesus in the Eucharist, and allow him to transform your own heart and mind to be more like his; 3) "Receive what you are; become what you receive."[15] This profound exhortation regarding the disposition with which we should receive the Eucharist was first formulated by Saint Augustine. Meditate deeply upon Augustine's insightful phrase, and strive to adopt this attitude every time you receive the Eucharist.

In the Eucharist, we receive the Body of Christ, incorporating us ever more fully into that Body, the Body to which we were first joined at Baptism. When we receive the Eucharist, Jesus abides in us, and we abide in him (John 6:56). Fortified by that divine food and drink, we are, in turn, to become the Body of Christ in the world. Like Jesus, we are to "break ourselves open and pour ourselves out" in love for our fellow human beings, becoming "food" and "drink" for them as they make their way through their own journey to Love.

12.

Love in Four (Not So) Easy Steps

To love someone is to be willing to give that person the gift of yourself. To love someone is to be willing to surrender yourself to that person. To love someone is to be willing to "break yourself open and pour yourself out" for that person. OK, that all sounds nice, but how do you actually *do* these things? How do you, in concrete terms, actually *love* someone else? Here's how to love, in four (not so) easy steps:

> Approve of the good in the other person
> Will the good of the other person
> Take action to help bring about the good of the other person
> Strive for unity and peace with the other person

No, these steps are not always easy to carry out. In many cases, they can actually be extremely difficult to carry out. But there's really no way around them. To learn to be a loving person, you have to learn to do these things for other people (and you have to learn to allow other people to do these things for you, too!). Are you doing these things for the people you claim to love? Do you allow other people to do these things for you?

13.

How Good that You Exist!

What does everyone want the most? Well, to be happy, of course. And happiness turns out to be inextricably intertwined with love, as we shall see. But what else do people want, besides happiness? *Approval.* Everyone wants approval from other people. Some people are more desirous of approval than others, and some people are more aware than others of the existence of this desire within themselves. But the fact is, we all want to be approved of by others. Even gang members want to be approved of (at least by other members of their gang). In fact, that's one of the main reasons that some adolescents seek out gang membership in the first place: to gain a sense of approval from their fellow gang members, to experience a sense of belonging and acceptance. Kids who experience approval at home, and who have a sense of belonging to a solid family, are far less likely to seek out a gang to join, and are far less likely to respond to a gang's efforts to recruit them.

So what does it mean to "approve" of someone? Literally, it means to judge that person to be *good*, in the sense of having *value* or *worth*.[16] We all want to be judged to be valuable. We all want to be judged as being worth something. Josef Pieper, the insightful Roman Catholic philosopher from Germany, described the type of approval we seek, and the type of approval that others seek from us, as being captured by the exclamation, "How good that you exist!" We want other people to be *glad* that we exist, and other people want us to be glad that they exist. We all want to feel like we *matter*, that the world would be diminished by our absence.

You cannot truly love another person if you cannot honestly proclaim that it is good that they exist. You cannot truly love another person if you cannot first see some good in them. Finding some good in the other person is the first essential step toward being able to love them. And once you have found that good, you then have to *continue* to see the good in them, even at times when you may find that very difficult to do. Otherwise, love dies.

14.

Where Love Is, There Is the Eye

How do you find, and then continue to see, the good in other people? Especially those people in your life who are particularly difficult to get along with, much less love? How does one love even the seemingly unlovable person? Well, first of all, you have to *want* to find some good in them. Finding and approving the good in other people is an act of your *will*. You have to *choose* to look for the good rather than the bad in others; you have to choose to *focus* on the good rather than the bad. As fallen creatures, we all tend to be a mixture of the good and the bad. To will to focus on the good more than the not-so-good in others is to open your heart more fully to love. Genuine love cannot take root when you are quicker to see the faults and shortcomings in others than you are to see the good in them.

There is a Latin phrase that applies here: *Ubi amor, ibi oculus* – "Where love is, there is the eye." Love enables us to *see*. Love enables us to see the *good* more clearly: in other people, in ourselves, and in life itself. (Love enables us to see *beauty* and *truth* more clearly as well – more about that later). Adopting a predisposition toward love by consciously willing to find the good in others actually makes it more possible for you to *see* the good that is there – the good that otherwise might have escaped your notice.

Adopting a predisposition toward love opens up our eyes, our minds, and our hearts to other people.

There's another old saying that is also relevant here: "People see what they want to see." Well, that's often true. Old sayings don't tend to become "old sayings" unless they have at least a grain (and often much more than a grain) of truth in them. People *do* tend to see what they want to see. If people choose to focus on the faults and shortcomings of other people, that's mostly what they will see in them. But thankfully, this phenomenon works in the other direction as well: if people choose to focus on the good in others, then they will mostly see the good. Resolve to focus on the good in others rather than the not-so-good, and to keep yourself focused on the good you find in them. When you find your attention drifting toward their faults, consciously re-direct your attention to the good. Like most things in the school of love, this becomes easier with practice. One of the reasons the most difficult people in your life are in your life is to help you practice things like this.

15.

There Are No Ordinary People

Unfortunately, *wanting* to see the good in other people may not be enough to enable you to actually see the good, especially the good in those people who can be more difficult to love. Finding and approving the good in other people is not just a matter of your will; it is also a matter of your *mind*, of the way you think of other people in general. What is your attitude toward other people? Are people basically good, or basically bad? Do all people have intrinsic value and worth, or are they only valuable if they are in some way useful to you – to the extent that they serve your purposes or needs, approve of *you*, agree with you on important issues, etc.? Being able to find, and to continue to see, the good in other people may require that you begin to think about people (*all* people) differently than you have in the past. It may require that you adopt a different attitude toward people. What kind of attitude? *God's* attitude. And what is God's attitude toward people? That people are *very good* (Genesis 1:31). God's proclamation that the first human beings were very good was, in part, God's way of saying "How good that you exist!" And God says that about each of us. Every one of us. Or else we wouldn't exist. It is God's love which created us, and it is God's love which sustains us in existence. All of us. Even that person you find to be so cantankerous, so petty, so annoying, etc. If God can exclaim about every person he created, "How good that you exist!", we should be able to find a way to do that, too.

God proclaims human beings to be very good because he made us *imago Dei*, in his image and likeness (Genesis 1:26). God made us like himself in our ability to think and reason, but he also made us like him in our ability to *love*. Everything that God created is *good* because it shares in God's being, the being of the Infinite Good. But human beings are *very* good because we share in God's capacity to love. Every single human being has intrinsic value and dignity because God loves them. Every single human being has intrinsic value and dignity because they were made *imago Dei*. Every single human being has intrinsic value and dignity because they were created to be a child of God. Every single human being has intrinsic value and dignity because they were created to share in, and contribute to, the eternal circulation of love that constitutes the divine life. Every single human being has intrinsic value and dignity because Jesus died and rose for them so that they could share in the life of God. Keeping these truths in mind will make it much more possible for you to find and approve of the good in other people.

Admittedly, some people, although made *imago Dei* in their capacity to love, don't seem to be exercising that capacity very much. But maybe part of our mission in this life is to help draw the capacity for love out of people who are like that, to draw the capacity for love out of that difficult person whom no one else seems to like very much, by first loving them. And loving them starts with finding some good in them. And finding some good in them starts with seeing them as being children of God. All of them. As C. S. Lewis put it, "There are no ordinary people."[17] We need to adopt that attitude toward *every* person who crosses our path in life.

16.

Lord, I Want to See

Most of us are not physically blind, but we all suffer from at least some degree of *spiritual* blindness. And one of the most common types of spiritual blindness is not being able (or willing) to see the good in other people. Striving to open our hearts and minds to see the good in every other human being is an important first step, but it's generally not enough. We need some help. Divine help. We need God's help to love in the deepest sense of the word. We need God's help to love as God loves. We need God to instill the divine love in us, to infuse us with the divine love, so that we can then love others with the divine love. And being able to love others as God loves them requires first and foremost that we be able to find and focus upon the good in each and every person. We all need to pray on a regular basis for that grace, especially with regard to the most difficult people and the most difficult situations in our lives. We need to pray for God to transform our way of looking at, and thinking about, other people. We need to pray for a God's-eye view, so to speak. We need to pray to be able to see with the eyes of Christ, who during his earthly life always saw the potential for good in people even when others could not. We need to pray for our hearts and minds to be transformed into the heart and mind of Christ. We all need to join with the blind beggar who repeatedly asked Jesus to help him as Jesus was passing by him on his way to Jericho. Touched by the man's persistence, Jesus stopped and asked him, "What do you want me to do for you?" The blind man immediately replied, "Lord, I want to see." (Luke 18:41; NIV). As people who are so often blind, whether willfully or inadvertently, to the good in others, let us join in the blind man's entreaty: *Lord, help us to see!*

17.

The Playwright and the Teacher

For some of us, the person we might need the most divine help to find and approve the good in is…God. This is really crucial: it is very difficult, if not impossible, to deeply love other people (especially those people whom we perceive as our "enemies") if we are unable, or unwilling, to see the good in the God who created those people in the first place and who sustains them in existence. Some of us may harbor lingering resentments or grudges against God that block our ability to see the infinite goodness in God and therefore block our ability to love God and other people: *God, how could you let that person whom I loved so much die? God, why didn't you answer that prayer request that was so important to me and for which I so earnestly prayed? God, why have you stood by while I have gone through so much pain and suffering in my life? God, why do you allow so much evil and suffering in this world?*

Not at all to belittle any of those hurts, disappointments, and frustrations, but they tend to flow from an overly narrow view of life (and of God). Some of them stem from a misunderstanding of who and what God is: God is not a magic genie who is there to grant our every wish. If you are a parent: do you give your kids every single thing they ask for, in exactly the way they ask for it, immediately after they ask for it? Hopefully not, because you are trying to raise healthy, mature adults, rather than adults who are "spoiled rotten", right? Something similar holds true with regard to God's treatment of us. God is seeking to raise healthy, mature adults who can love as he loves so that they can share forever in the divine life and bliss. Doing so requires that God sometimes deny us things that we mistakenly think would be best for us.

Some of these complaints against God flow from a misunderstanding of what *life* is all about. Life is a beautiful, grand drama of love. Life is also a difficult, demanding school of love. But there is no drama if our choices do not have any real consequences, including the risk that we may use our freedom to choose to do evil to each other in this life, and the risk of negative consequences from the bad choices we make. And we cannot really learn how to love without being willing to undergo the pain and suffering that can come with the self-sacrifice that lies at the heart of love.

To be able to love other people deeply, we need to get to a place where we can honestly exclaim to God: How good that you exist! How beautiful this life and this world are that you have created! How good that you have created all of us (*all* of us) to be members of the Body of Christ, to share in the divine life and love!

It's difficult to enjoy the play, and to get the most out of it, if you are always criticizing and complaining about the Playwright. And it's difficult to get a good education if all you do is complain about your Teacher.

18.

God's Bright Image of You

Yes, for some of us, the person we have the most trouble seeing and approving of the good in is God. But for others of us, that person is *ourselves*. And if we cannot see much (or even any) good in ourselves, we are definitely going to find it difficult to see and approve of the good in others.

Admittedly, the claim that many of us have difficulty seeing and approving of the good in ourselves may seem counterintuitive these days: we live in what is almost certainly the most self-centered, self-focused era in human history; how can it possibly be that many of us have trouble seeing and approving of the good in ourselves? Well, one could argue that it is precisely *because* so many people do not see any good in themselves that our society has become so self-focused. Many people in our society feel empty inside; their lives do not seem to them to have any ultimate meaning or purpose. Their lives feel pointless. Their lives do not seem to *matter* to anyone, to make any sort of difference in the world. Some people strive to fill up that emptiness in a variety of ways: money, sex, possessions, status, fame, etc. Others seek to escape from the feelings of meaninglessness and emptiness via drugs or alcohol.

If only all of us could see ourselves (and life itself) through *God's* eyes, through the eyes of *Christ*. In the mind and heart of

God, there is a "bright image"[18] of each of us, of each and every person God has ever created: an image of who and what God created each person to be; an image of the unique mission of love for which that person was created. Our lives *do* have ultimate meaning and purpose. Life itself has an ultimate meaning and purpose.

One of our missions as Christians is to help others see God's "bright image" of them, to see the good, and the potential for good, in themselves, and to help them actualize that potential. But to be able to do that, we need to make sure that we are able to see God's "bright image" of us, too.

19.

The Creative Power of Love

Love is creative. Love is transformative. Love can create something good that was not there before. Love can take what *is* there and transform it into something better.

The Christian faith teaches that God created the universe *ex nihilo:* out of nothing. Not out of some pre-existing primordial matter, but out of *nothing.* Stop for a moment and let that sink in. The entire cosmos, everything that exists in the universe, all created out of *nothingness.* How could that be? How could God possibly have created everything that exists, including ourselves, out of nothingness? By the creative power of love. That is why the Christian faith also teaches that God created the universe *ex amore:* out of love. Love can make be. Love can bring something into existence that did not exist before. Finding and approving of the good in other people (and ourselves) is actually a form of participation in creation, in God's creative power, because it is a participation in God's creative love.

Purely human love can be transformative (as exemplified, at a simple level, by what has been referred to as the "Pygmalion effect"), but just think of what love can do when it is the divine love flowing through us, the divine love that created everything that exists and sustains everything in being from moment to moment! If we take the time and effort to look carefully, we can see goodness in other people that we may never have noticed before. In fact, we can sometimes see goodness in them that *they* have never noticed before! We may even be able to see goodness in them that is not actually there yet! When we look at another person with an open mind and an open heart, we can see into the possible future. We can catch a glimpse of God's bright image of that person. We can catch sight of the God-given potential for goodness in that person, a vision of who and what God created that person to be. We can see that person, at least partially, through God's eyes. And when we communicate that goodness to the person in whom we see it, when we convey our *approval* of the goodness we see in that person, that approval can transform them. That approval, that encouragement of the good and the potential for good in the other person, can cause them to blossom and thrive like never before. Some parents know this. Some teachers know this. Some coaches know this. They have seen it happen firsthand. In fact, one of the most rewarding experiences one can ever have as a parent, as a teacher, or as a coach, is to watch something good and beautiful appear in your child, in your student, in your athlete, that was not there before, or that was at best partial and undeveloped, in response to your approval and your encouragement of that person.

God has given each of us the incredible privilege, and the serious responsibility, of participating in the creative, transformative power of love. Take the time today to stop and notice the goodness in at least one person, and to praise them for that goodness. You just might transform someone's life.

20.

More than a Feeling

One of the most common misconceptions regarding love is that love is mainly about *emotion*, about how one *feels* toward another person. People are especially likely to believe that this is the case with romantic love. This misunderstanding of the true nature of love may be one of the factors contributing to the rise in the divorce rate in recent decades. Some people assume that if they don't feel "warm and fuzzy feelings" toward their spouse most of the time, then they must not be "in love" with their spouse any more, and that it's time to move on to someone else who *does* spark those feelings.

But genuine love is not just about emotion; in fact, genuine love is not even *primarily* a matter of emotion. Love is a matter of the *will*. Love is a matter of *choosing* to love another person, and *continuing* to choose to love that person, even at times when you may not be feeling many (or even *any*) "warm and fuzzy feelings" toward them. Sure, it makes it much easier to "love" someone when you feel lots of positive sentiments toward them. But love is not mainly about those sentiments. Resolving to continue to love your spouse through thick and thin is one of the keys to keeping love in a marriage, and to making a marriage last. But it is not just romantic love that is primarily a matter of will; so are all other forms of genuine love.

To love someone is to *choose* to offer the gift of one's self to that person in a way that is fitting to the nature of the relationship, whether that person is your spouse, your child, a friend, a co-worker, a "neighbor" (whether literal or figurative), or even some-one you perceive to be your "enemy". The four key elements of self-gift are all matters of the *will*: one has to *will* to make the ef-fort to find and approve of the good in the other person; one has to *will* the good of that person; one has to *will* to take action to help bring about their good; and one has to *will* to strive for unity and peace with that person. Positive emotions (including deep and lasting joy) can, and often do, result from these actions of the will. But those emotions are the *consequences* of love rather than the *essence* of love. To love is to *will* to love.

21.

Ut in Deo Sit

If one of the key elements of loving another person is to will that person's good, what exactly does that mean? Well, of course, willing their good can include willing that they be happy; that they be healthy and well; that good things will happen to them; that good things will come their way; etc. But the deepest love you can have for someone is to will their *ultimate* good. And what is their ultimate good? What is every single human being's ultimate good? *Ut in Deo sit*: that they may be in God. To will someone's ultimate good is to will that they might reach their intended destiny, the destiny for which they were made: to be in God, to share forever in the eternal circulation of love that is the divine life. Thus, to will someone's ultimate good is to will that they might choose Love. To will someone's ultimate good is to will that they might say Yes to their God-given mission of love and fulfill that mission in their lives. To will someone's ultimate good is to will that they might excel in the school of love, continuing to grow in their ability to love selflessly as their life progresses. To will someone's ultimate good is to will that they might grow into God's "bright image" of them.

Keeping the beloved's ultimate good in mind and heart will guide you as you strive to will the good for them at specific times and in specific circumstances of their lives. To will their good at any point in time is to will whatever will help them learn to love God and neighbor more deeply. To will their good is to will whatever will help them to say Yes to their mission of love. To will their good is to will whatever will help them fulfill that mission. To will their good is to will whatever will help them to excel in the school of love, to will whatever will help them to grow in their ability to selflessly give and receive the gift of self in love. To will their good is to will whatever will help them take another step toward becoming the loving person God created them to be. To will their good is to will whatever will help them be *in God*.

In a happy coincidence (actually, it's not a coincidence at all), to will all of that for the beloved is simultaneously to will their ultimate happiness, and to will that they find a profound sense of meaning and purpose in life, and to will that they be free, and to will that they be at peace. For the fulfillment of all of those deepest desires of their heart is ultimately to be found in Love.

22.

Tough Love

Genuine love is demanding. Genuine love makes demands on the beloved, precisely *because* love wills the good of the beloved. Genuine love sets high expectations for the beloved, because love wants the beloved to grow into the person they were created to be, to reach the full potential that the lover sees in them but that the beloved may not even be able to see in themselves. This holds true, first and foremost, with regard to God's love for each of us. God views each of us through the lens of his "bright image" of us, his image of the deeply loving person he created us to be, the deeply loving person who has mastered the lessons in the school of love and is ready to enter fully into the eternal circulation of love. God calls us to a very high standard ("love your enemies"; "deny yourself"; "take up your cross"; etc.), not because God derives pleasure from being tough on us; but because being "tough" on us will help form and shape us into people who can love as God loves and thereby share most fully in the divine bliss of self-giving love.

Some of us wish for a God who weren't so demanding, a God who didn't have such high expectations. Some of us wish for a weak, wishy-washy Jesus who makes no demands on us and approves of us no matter what. They want to focus on the initial part of Jesus' statement to the sinner ("Has no one condemned you?

Neither do I condemn you") and to leave out the final, but absolutely essential, part of that statement: "Go, and do not sin again." (John 8:3-11) As C. S. Lewis pointed out, some of us wish for a God who is like a senile uncle or grandparent, a God who "just likes to see people have a good time." In other words, a God who leaves us alone and lets us do whatever we feel like doing. But as Lewis also points out, to wish for a God like that is actually to wish for less love, not more. To wish for a God like that is also to wish to *be* less. God calls us to be *more*.

Our human loves are to imitate the divine love in this, as in all other facets of the divine love. Good parents know this. Good parents know to set firm rules for their children's behavior and to insist that those rules be obeyed. Good parents know to set high (but reasonable and achievable) standards for their children, including, first and foremost, standards regarding loving God and neighbor selflessly. Good parents know to hold their children to those standards. There may be moments when kids (especially teenagers) complain about those rules and standards, but deep down, most kids (even teenagers, though they may be reluctant to admit it) *want* those rules and standards because they know that those rules and standards are a sign of their parents' love for them. Parents must set rules and expectations for their children if they are to fulfill their role of helping to shape and form those children into God's bright image of them.

One of the main purposes of marriage is for the spouses to help each other make their way through the school of love. One of the reasons your spouse is here is to help you grow into God's bright image of you. And one of the reasons *you're* here is to help your spouse grow into God's bright image of them. Agree to call each other out (privately, tactfully, gently, constructively, lovingly) when one of you sees the other being less loving toward other people than they could be. Good spouses do this for each other. Good spouses are open to their spouse doing this for them. By the way, did I mention you need to do this *privately, tactfully, gently, constructively, and lovingly*?

In imitating the divine love in placing demands on the beloved and setting high standards for the beloved, it's best to start with self-love. Demand more of yourself. Strive harder to grow into God's bright image of you. Strive harder to grow in your ability to give and receive the gift of self in love. Strive to do a better job of loving your spouse. Strive to do a better job of loving your kids. Strive to do a better job of loving your perceived "enemies". Remove the beam from your own eye, and then you will be better able to remove the splinter from your neighbor's eye (Luke 6:41-42).

23.

It's Tough to Love

Yes, genuine love is demanding on the beloved. But genuine love tends to be even more demanding on the *lover*. Willing the good of the beloved sometimes means letting go of your *own* will for them, especially when your will for them does not align with what is for their ultimate good. But that's what love does: sacrifice for the sake of the beloved.

If spouses don't already know this, they better learn it pretty quickly if they want to keep their marriage healthy and happy. Your spouse will not always fit neatly into your own plans for yourself and for your marriage. Your spouse has their own hopes and dreams, the pursuit of which may cause some disruption of your own plans. Your spouse also has a God-given mission, whatever that may be, and one of your roles as their spouse is to will that they be able to fulfill that mission, and to help make that possible for them. You may need to let go of some of what you willed for them, for yourself, or for your marriage in order to help make their mission, and their other hopes and dreams, possible. In the strongest marriages, your spouse will be willing to do the same for you. But usually, one or the other has to set the example in this. Do this for your spouse.

Similarly, good parents realize that willing the ultimate good for their children sometimes requires that they sacrifice their own, often more short-sighted, will for them. As a parent, you might wish that your child would follow in the footsteps of your own career, or that they would choose to marry this person rather than that one, or that they would choose to settle near you as an adult so that you can see them often. But some or all of *your* wishes for your child may not align with *God's* will for your child, nor with the path that will lead your child to the fulfillment of their God-given mission. How tenaciously we tend to cling to our own will for our kids, sometimes not only to the detriment of our children, but even to our own detriment! Maybe you "succeed" in the short run in persuading your daughter or son to marry the person *you* prefer; but was it worth it if your daughter or son eventually rebels against your undue influence and cuts off contact with you? Be willing to let go of your own preferences for your children when those preferences seem likely to conflict with your children's *ultimate* good.

24.

Sacrum Facere

Sooner or later, love presents the would-be lover with a choice, a choice that cannot be avoided. The choice involves the issue of *sacrifice*: do you love this other person enough to sacrifice for them? Are you willing to give up something that is very important to you for the sake of the beloved? Are you willing to be inconvenienced, go out of your way, maybe even go to great lengths to *take action* to help bring about the good of the beloved? Love is tested by *sacrifice*.[19]

Sure, the first two elements of loving self-gift (approving the good in the other person and willing the good of the other person) can be difficult at times. But the third element of self-gift, taking action to help bring about the good of the other person, is where the rubber really hits the road.

How can someone *know* that you truly love them? Is it enough for you to *tell* them that you love them? Well, it helps, of course, and people need to hear this from you (hopefully often). We *all* need to hear that we are loved, since we were all born for love and crave love. But we also know that "talk is cheap", and saying something does not necessarily make it so. Saying the words "I love you" isn't enough. Nor is it enough to will the other person's good: "If a brother or sister is poorly clothed and in lack of daily food, and one of you says to them, 'Go in peace, be warmed and filled,' without giving them the things needed for the body, what does it profit?" (James 2:15-16).

It can be relatively easy to *wish* someone well, as long as it does not require any further action on our part. No, the proof of love lies in *doing* something to help bring about the good of the beloved, especially something that requires some sort of sacrifice on your part. Sometimes, the action required may be for you to let go of your *own* will for the beloved, especially when your will for them does not align with what is for their ultimate good. Sometimes, you might need to sacrifice some of your own hopes or dreams for your own life for the sake of the beloved's good. People who have been married for any significant length of time have generally confronted such a choice. And most parents have faced such choices for the sake of their children. It's not easy to choose the self-sacrificial path in life. But that's what genuine love does. Genuine love is willing to sacrifice for the sake of the beloved.

Sacrifice lies at the heart of love, because love is all about the gift of self, and the deepest gift of self involves sacrificing something important to oneself for the sake of the beloved. The etymology of the word "sacrifice" yields a crucial insight here. The English word "sacrifice" is derived from the Latin phrase *sacrum facere*, which means "to make holy".[20] Sacrifice *makes holy*. When we sacrifice for the sake of another person, that sacrifice *makes us holy*. But what does it mean to be "holy"? To be holy is to be *like God*. A sacrifice made in the name of love makes us holy, makes us more like God, because God *is* self-sacrificing love. That's why God exhorts us, "Be holy, for I am holy" (Leviticus 11:44, 19:2,

20:7; 1 Peter 1:16): the more fully we enter into the dynamic of self-sacrificial love in this life, the more like God we become, and thus the more deeply we will be able to share in God's divine life.

The fullness of being, the fullness of life, the *divine* life: these are all synonymous, and they all consist in one thing: *giving*. That can be hard for us to hear. It can be hard for us to believe. But it's the Truth, with a capital "T". Many of us are convinced that ultimate happiness, the fullness of life, is found in *having*, not giving, so we spend much, if not all, of our lives grabbing everything we can for ourselves. Having enriches us, but giving depletes us, we think. But it turns out that giving and having are not mutually exclusive. In fact, they turn out to be intimately interconnected. In one of the most beautiful paradoxes in the drama of love that is this life, *giving* actually leads to *having*. Having lies on the far side of giving. When we give, we end up having, too. But the giving has to come first.

> Until you learn to give deeply of your self, you will never know the deepest possible love.
>
> Until you learn to give deeply of your self, you will never know the greatest possible happiness.
>
> Until you learn to give deeply of your self, you will never know the deepest possible meaning and purpose in life.
>
> Until you learn to give deeply of your self, you will never know the greatest possible freedom.
>
> Until you learn to give deeply of your self, you will never know the greatest possible peace.

To find your life, you must indeed first lose it (Luke 17:33): in the self-sacrificial gift of self, given in love. Give until it hurts, and then give some more. The pain and suffering you may temporarily experience are merely the pain that comes from the shattering of the shell of your ego, the pain that comes with dying to your false self. On the far side of the pain and suffering of self-sacrificial love lies your true self, God's bright image of you. On the far side of the pain and suffering of self-sacrificial love lies the bliss of the divine life and love.

25.

E Pluribus Unum

The claim that ultimate happiness lies along the path of self-sacrificial love, and *only* there, flies in the face of much of pop psychology, and certainly in the face of much of the advertising to which we are exposed, both of which tend to claim that focusing on one*self* is the path to happiness and fulfillment. But focusing entirely, or even mostly, on yourself will never make you truly and lastingly happy. Because your ego just isn't big enough to satisfy you. And trying to make your ego bigger through more accomplishments, more money, more power, more fame, etc. won't help in the long run, either. Because you weren't made for your ego. You were made for love, you were made for connectedness, you were made for relationship. You were made to share in the divine life, and the divine life is all about relationship. The divine life *is* relationship. The divine life is all about union and unity among the three divine Persons in the *one* God: Father, Son, and Holy Spirit. You were made to share in that union with God and with all other human beings. What's the ultimate goal of this drama that is our earthly life? *E pluribus unum*: out of the many, one. Not a *numerical* one; we don't get *absorbed* into God or into other human beings. No, our intended destiny is the oneness of being united in love, the oneness of *union,* the oneness of *communion.*

That's why the fourth and final element of love as self-gift is the *desire for union with the other* and the willingness to strive to bring about that union. Love is not complete, love is not perfected, without this desire for union. How can you claim to "love" someone if you aren't really willing to be closely connected to them, to have a relationship with them, to share yourself with them and have them share themselves with you, to be in *communion* with them?

We're all hard-wired for relationship, for union with God and neighbor. That's why discord and dissension are so stressful for us; they run counter to our gut instinct for what life is supposed to be like. Ultimately, life is meant to be lived in peace and harmony, not division and discord. In fact, one of our deepest desires in life is the desire for this deep and abiding peace. But ultimate peace is found only in union and unity: in the union and unity of love.

PART III

THE TWO MOVEMENTS OF LOVE

26.

Hell Is the Refusal to Love

"Hell is...other people." Jean-Paul Sartre, the French existentialist philosopher, wrote this line in his play entitled *No Exit.*[21] Presumably, Sartre penned this line with an eye toward the pain and suffering we human beings sometimes inflict on each other: little slights, outright insults, malicious gossip, physical assaults, rape, murder...the list goes on and on. But Sartre's statement goes far beyond the truism that we sometimes inflict pain on each other. The intensity of the statement, it could be argued, seems to suggest a desire for a world without other people, a belief that "Life would be better if it weren't for other people."

A similar sentiment might lie behind the claims made by some Eastern religions that multiplicity is bad, that multiplicity is illusion, and that the only true reality is the one universal consciousness. "Salvation" lies in seeing through the illusion of multiplicity and realizing one's unity with (indeed, one's *identity* with) the one universal consciousness.

There is at least a grain of truth in such teachings: namely, that we human beings were made for union and unity. However, we were not made for a unity achieved by our dissolution as individuals, by our absorption into a single universal consciousness that obliterates our individuality. We were made for a unity achieved through *love*. Love bridges the differences (and the distance) between us in order to bring about union and unity, but without destroying our individuality. One Body, with many members.

Distance, difference, otherness: rather than being bad things or illusions to be seen through, these are actually *good* things. Distance, difference, and otherness are good things because they *make love possible*. Recall that love is the selfless gift of self, *given and received*. Love is not possible without distance, without difference, without otherness. Without these, there can be no loving exchange of the gift of self. First and foremost, this is true within the divine life of God; in order for God's essence to be love, there must be "otherness" within God: the "otherness", the "distance", the "difference" that exists between Father, Son, and Holy Spirit.[22] Acting out of the divine love and freedom, God also makes space for us human beings, and all of creation, within the space that exists between the Father and the Son.[23] The fact that we are different from, and other than, God, is good, for it makes love possible between God and us; God calls the world very good, even in its difference from God (Gen 1:31).[24] The difference between us and God makes it possible for us to enter into a loving union with God while still retaining our identities as unique persons. In our union with God, our individuality is not dissolved, but preserved within the otherness that is integral to the divine life.[25]

This "unity-in-difference" also holds true of love between human beings. Our difference from other human beings (i.e., our "non-identity" with them) makes possible the exchange of the gift of self and therefore loving union between human beings. We don't desire to be absorbed into the beloved; we desire *union* with them.[26]

So Sartre was wrong when he wrote that "Hell is other people." Yes, the differences between us can sometimes lead to dissension and discord, even violence, but those very differences are also what make love possible, the greatest good of all. John Milton, the English poet, was far closer to the truth than Sartre when he wrote "Myself am hell."[27] rather than "Hell is other people". Hell is choosing to close myself up within the cramped confines of my ego rather than opening myself up to give and receive the gift of self in love. Hell is choosing self over other. Hell is the refusal to love.[28]

27.

The Primacy of Receptivity

Because you exist, you have already been the recipient of the loving gift of self – from God. All of us have. All of us who exist have been given the incalculable gift of a share in God's being, the gift of existence itself. Genuine love involves two movements: both the giving and the receiving of the gift of self, or what I like to refer to as donativity (from the Greek word *donare,* meaning "to give") and receptivity. But for us human beings, receptivity always comes first: This is love, not that we have loved God, but that God has first loved us (1 John 4:10). All human beings, all creatures, all created things, are the recipients of God's love in that they all receive the gift of their existence from the Source of all being. God's essence is to give, and all created things are the beneficiaries of the divine generosity.

But we human beings have been given the additional gift of being made in God's image and likeness in our ability to love. We are not just the *recipients* of love; we have been given the ability to pass the divine love on to others. We are called to become givers, not just receivers. But the receiving has to come first. To be able to give, you first have to open yourself up to receive. The more we open ourselves up to receive the divine love, the more love we have to pass on to others. Receptivity fuels donativity. Ultimately, all of our giving is fueled by the divine giving.

The Primacy of Receptivity

28.

Diastole and Systole

Our hearts beat according to the rhythm of diastole and systole; our lives are meant to follow that same rhythm. As red blood cells in the Body of Christ, we draw our supply of oxygen (the divine love) from the divine heart and lungs. The Sacred Heart of Jesus then contracts and sends us out to all the other members and prospective members of that Body so we can share that life-giving oxygen with them. We inhale the divine love so we can exhale that love to all the people with whom we come into contact. Then, spent and depleted, we circle back to the divine heart and lungs, to be replenished and strengthened and energized by the divine love once again.

The rhythm of our lives is meant to alternate between resting in God and action in the world. Contemplation feeds and sustains action, and action feeds and sustains contemplation. Prayer and loving action are synergistic, intimately and inextricably interconnected. Receptivity fuels donativity, which in turn fuels greater receptivity. Receive, give, repeat: the rhythm of our lives. It is in this rhythm of receiving and giving that we find our deepest joy.

29.

From and For

We all exist from and for. We all exist from others and for others. We were made for relationship, for connection. We were made to live forever in that space between from and for.

First, our "from-ness": Now, more than ever before in human history, we find our very existence, not to mention our daily comfort, to be dependent on the labor of others. Most of the goods and services that sustain us in our daily lives come from other people. Most of us take this fact (and the people who provide those goods and services) for granted. The Covid-19 pandemic brought this interdependency to some people's attention for the first time, as they considered such possibilities as "What if the supply chains to grocery stores for many foods are broken, and I can't buy the food I need?" and "What if I contract the virus and the hospitals are so full that they just don't have any room for me?" and "What if the countries that supply many of our antibiotics and other medicines cut off that supply?" The reality is that our lives are highly dependent on each other; we all live "from" each other, like it or not.

But at an even more fundamental level, we all exist "from" in that we all come from God and are sustained in existence from moment to moment by God, who sustains *all* things in existence: not just us human beings, but also all of those things that we depend on for life: oxygen, the heat and light provided by the sun, the seeds that grow into plants and fruit that we can eat, etc.

Some of us want to throw off what we see as being the shackles of relationships, including our "from-ness". We want to be completely in-dependent from others (especially from God); then we'll be completely free, we think. But true freedom is found *in* relationships, not out of them. We can try to run from our "from-ness", but there's really no escape from "from". Better to embrace our "from-ness" than to fight it.

Because when we embrace our "from-ness", we're better equipped for our "for-ness". We were made for for-ness. God is, first and foremost, *for* others. Jesus Christ revealed God's "for-ness" to us in no uncertain terms. Jesus' life (and his death) were entirely *for* others. (By the way, Jesus also completely accepted his "from-ness" as well: read the Gospel of John and notice how many times Jesus says that he comes *from* the Father or was sent *by* the Father.) As creatures made in the image and likeness of God, we are to be "for" others just as God is "for" others.

Some of us want to reject that "for-ness", mostly because of the demands that "being for" others places on us. Thomas Nagel, one of the more intellectually honest and candid of the people publicly proclaiming their atheism in recent years, admits that his atheism does not just involve his belief that there is no God; it also stems from his *desire* that there not be a God. Nagel admits to a "cosmic authority problem", saying he "doesn't want the universe to be that way". But the truth is, our lives are not entirely our own, even though we might want to believe they are. Our lives are meant to be *for* others, and others' lives are meant to be *for* others, including *for* us. If we would all cooperate in that, it would work out beautifully. Because that's the divine plan, that's God's intention for his creation, that's the whole point of the drama of our lives: that we all might choose to dwell in the space between from and for. And that space lies precisely within the Body of Christ, the God-man who most fully embodies from-ness and for-ness.

30.

Open on Both Sides

One of the essential prerequisites for dwelling in the space between from and for, one of the essential prerequisites for giving and receiving the gift of self in love, is *openness*. In this regard (as, indeed, in *all* regards), Jesus is the archetypal human being, the model we are called to imitate. Jesus is the first completely open human being, completely open to God and completely open to his fellow human beings.[29] Jesus is open "vertically" toward God, frequently retreating to spend time in prayer with God during his earthly life and always focused on carrying out the will of the Father, which is always love. And Jesus is open "horizontally" toward his "neighbor", toward all his fellow human beings. So open, in fact, that he scandalized some of the other members of his society: How could Jesus speak with, even *socialize* with, people they deemed to be the dregs of their society: outcasts like tax collectors and prostitutes and other sinners? In this, Jesus was revealing both the divine openness of God to *all* his children (especially those who have lost their way) and the human openness to which each of us is called. Jesus is "open on both sides": fully open to both the giving and the receiving of the gift of self.

Saint Augustine once defined sin as being *incurvatus in sei*: being *closed in* on oneself. It's a concise formulation. Sin is withdrawing completely inside one's ego and caring only about one's own needs and desires. Sin is focusing entirely on oneself, to the exclusion of God and neighbor. Sin is a lack of love.[30] Sin is constructing walls around your ego to keep God and other people out. At first, it might feel pretty good in there. Safe. Familiar. Comfortable. But sooner or later, it starts to feel pretty empty in there. Sooner or later, it starts to get mighty lonely in there. We were "created open", made for openness, created to share in the divine openness. Self-enclosure stunts our growth. Our supplies grow thin; the air grows stale. Cut off from Love and love, we begin to atrophy. We begin to die. And why wouldn't we? We have chosen to cut ourselves off from the divine flow of love; we have chosen to cut ourselves off from the very Source of life itself. Myself am hell, indeed.

Some of us open up, but only partially. We may still attend Mass weekly, but how much do we let the Eucharist, and the Word of God, influence the way we live our lives the rest of the week? Or we may be heavily involved in social justice activities, striving mightily to improve the lives of others, but we have largely shut ourselves off from God, thinking we can build a better world entirely on our own. We no longer feel the need to attend Mass. We no longer feel the need to spend time with God in prayer. Soon, we may no longer feel the need for God at all.

Open up! Open your mind to the profound and amazing truth that it's all about love. Open your heart to the flow of the divine love, the love that so eagerly desires to course through you, fill you up, and overflow to the other people in your life. Open yourself up to be a channel of the divine love in the world. Open yourself up to give and receive the gift of self in love.

31.

Open or Closed?

The most important choice you will ever make in your life is not which person to marry. It's not what career to pursue. It's not where you choose to live. The most important choice you will ever make in your life is whether to open yourself up to, or to close yourself off from, the divine love. To close yourself off to God and God's love is to cut yourself off from the ultimate Source of life and love; the ultimate Source of happiness, meaning, freedom, peace, beauty, goodness, and truth; the very Ground of your existence. So why would anyone do that?

Some people protest that they're just too *busy*, that they don't have time for God, for prayer, for going to Mass, for reading the Bible, or anything else like that. But those people will find, if they carve out some time for their relationship with God, that their lives actually become calmer, less frantic, more manageable, more *peaceful*.

And then there are some people who *deliberately* make their lives as busy and as hectic as possible by continuously cramming more work, more activities, more events, etc. into their already jam-packed schedule. Often, such people are striving to fill up their schedules in a desperate attempt to fill up themselves. If they can just stay busy enough (they hope), they can avoid confronting the emptiness that they feel deep down inside, can avoid thinking about those nagging questions like "Is this all there is?"; "Why does my life feel so meaningless?"; "What's life all about?"; etc. Busy-ness and distraction might make such issues go away temporarily, but only temporarily.

Other people close themselves off from the divine love out of a mistaken sense of *pride*. They want to be entirely self-sufficient: not needing anybody else (certainly not God!), not depending on anyone for anything. Sometimes it takes a shock, a crisis of some sort, to jar such people out of their illusion of self-sufficiency. Maybe it's the loss of their job; maybe it's a serious car crash, maybe it's a life-threatening illness. Sometimes only such crises can force us to examine our priorities in life, our answers to the "big questions" of life. We can choose to allow suffering to draw us more deeply into love, or we can choose to let suffering drive us further away from love.

At the other end of the spectrum from the excessively proud are those who feel a debilitating sense of *shame*: "God could never forgive all of the terrible things I've done," they think. "God could never love someone like me." As a result, they, too, choose to close themselves off from God's love. But they're wrong, on both counts (see, for example, Isaiah 1:18-20 and Luke 15:11-32). No sin is too big for the infinitely loving and merciful God to forgive. God *wants* to forgive their sins and welcome them (or welcome them back) into the Body of Christ.

But perhaps the most common reason for closing one's heart to God and to the divine love is…*laziness* (also known as "acedia" or "sloth"). In our weaker moments, we would like to avoid the demands of love. We don't want to put ourselves out for others. We don't want to sacrifice for the sake of others. And we certainly don't want to "die to self". But to seek to avoid the demands of love is to settle for being less than what we were made to be, to settle for being less than what we are capable of becoming. It's not enough to just "muddle through" life. We're called to be *saints*; we're called to be transformed into Jesus Christ, the first completely open human being; we're called to be *love*.

Sometimes it's a combination of two or more of these factors (or other factors as well) that causes us to close ourselves off to the divine love. Admittedly, most of us don't close ourselves off completely to God, but all of us are less open to the divine love and the divine life than we are capable of being, and are therefore less fully *alive*, and less fully *loving*, than we could be. The more you close yourself off from the divine love, the less love you have to pass on to others, and the less alive you are. As Bishop Robert Barron would say, "That's just a law of spiritual physics!" Fortunately, the converse is also true: the more you open yourself up to God, the more God can share his love with you, and the more love you will then have to pass on to others, and the more fully *alive* you will be. So: open or closed? The choice is up to you....

32.

Ripples in the Pond

Have you ever thrown a rock into a totally placid pond and watched the ripples spread farther and farther outward, maybe all the way to the edge of the pond? One small stone can have an impact on the entire pond. Each of our actions is like a small stone thrown into the sea of humanity, having ripple effects that extend only God knows how far. An angry, hurtful action toward one's spouse can ripple into other people's lives as that spouse, reeling from hurt feelings, acts insensitively toward a co-worker, who then goes home and vents their resulting anger and frustration on *their* spouse, etc. Thankfully, though, loving actions can have such ripple effects as well. These facts alone should certainly give us pause as we reflect on the possible ripple effects of our actions, both past and present.

But that's not all. Our actions can have a *direct* impact on people who are physically distant from us (even on the other side of the world!), without having to ripple through innumerable other people to reach them. God can take the positive effects of our loving actions and pass those effects directly to another person anywhere in the world – for example, someone who is going through a very difficult time and who desperately needs some love and support. That person may find that they inexplicably have a sudden burst of energy and strength that enables them to cope with the crisis in their life. (God, being love, only passes on the effects of our *loving* actions, not our evil or hurtful actions, in this way.) In the Catholic tradition, these positive "effects" of loving actions are referred to as "merits" or "fruit".[31] Loving action bears fruit, and anyone in the world can be the beneficiary of that fruit through God's intermediation. We human beings are all interconnected to each other as current and prospective members of the Body of Christ, as current and prospective members of the *communio sanctorum* – the communion of saints. God can take the merits of your loving action and confer them on someone you've never met who might live halfway around the world from you!

Thomas Merton liked to say that we human beings are all connected to, and united with, each other at that small, still point in each of us where we are all being sustained by God in existence from moment to moment. God uses those points of connection to spread the benefits of our loving actions to other people. *You* have likely been the beneficiary of the loving actions of strangers through this beautiful and mysterious process that Balthasar has referred to as spiritual "osmosis".[32]

But that's still not all. Because God transcends time, God can take the merits of our loving actions and apply those benefits to people not only anywhere in the world, but to people from the past or future as well as the present. The circulation of spiritual goods in the communion of saints – the circulation of love – transcends both space and time. The two movements of love – the giving and the receiving of the gift of self – are forever taking place in the *communio sanctorum*. What a beautiful and meaningful life, in which every act of love, no matter how small, radiates into eternity for the benefit of others!

You'll never know (in this life, anyway) the ripple effects of your loving (and unloving) actions. What kind of waves are you making as you move through the school of love?

PART IV

THE VIRTUE OF SELFLESSNESS

33.

The Virtue of Selflessness

The most important choice confronting us in life can be framed in a variety of ways: love vs. the refusal to love; openness vs. closure to the divine love; transcendence of one's ego vs. withdrawal into one's ego; being for oneself vs. being for others; selflessness vs. selfishness. Over fifty years ago, Ayn Rand wrote a book called *The Virtue of Selfishness*. The book was intended to be somewhat countercultural at the time it was published. Rand was advocating selfishness as a positive quality, even a *virtue*, at a time when selfishness was still considered to be a *vice* by the majority of people in our society. Today, in contrast, selfishness is taken as a given by most people. Of course everyone's selfish; why shouldn't they be? Life's all about looking out for #1, right? Today, it would be countercultural to write a book entitled *The Virtue of Selfless-ness*. Only fools (and people striving to be faithful Christians – which is synonymous with fools, in some people's opinion) would strive to be self*less*. But as we have seen, selflessness, not selfishness, is the path to ultimate fulfillment, because selflessness is the essence of the divine life. The less self*ish* we become, the more self*less* we become, the more we come to resemble God. And the more we come to resemble God, the more deeply we can share in the divine life. Which is the point of the whole drama.

34.

Transcende Teipsum!

We all want to be part of something bigger than ourselves. Some of us find at least a partial fulfillment of this desire in our marriage and/or our family. Some find it in their work. Some find it in their friendships. Some find it by being active in a political party or movement. Some find this sense of belonging, this transcendence of self, in something as seemingly prosaic as being a rabid fan of a particular sports team, united with other fans in their love and support for the team.

But the truth is, none of these connections, none of these affiliations, can fully satisfy our desire to be part of something bigger than ourselves. Because ultimately, we want to be part of the biggest thing out there (so to speak): God. We want to be *in God*. That's one of the reasons why the greatest good we can will for others (and ourselves) is *ut in Deo sit*: that they (and we) may be in God.

But to be in God, we have to get out of ourselves. We can't be in God while still remaining ensconced in our egos. To be in God, we have to strive to become like God. And God is not self-enclosure; God is openness. God is not self*ish*ness; God is selfless-ness. We have to take the risk of venturing out of our ego, stepping out in love toward God and neighbor. We have to take the risk of opening ourselves up to receive and give the gift of self in love. We can't be a part of the *communio sanctorum* without transcending ourselves. We can't be a part of the Body of Christ without transcending ourselves. We can't be *in God* without transcending ourselves. That's why Saint Augustine repeatedly exhorted us: *Transcende teipsum!* Transcend yourself!

35.

Your Ego Isn't Big Enough

Yes, we all want to be part of something bigger than ourselves, because we are all hard-wired with an innate desire for God. But some of us mistakenly think that our ultimate fulfillment lies, not in being part of something bigger than ourselves, but in making *ourselves* bigger: bigger via more money, more power, more status, maybe some fame (even if it only lasts fifteen minutes), etc. But it won't work. No matter how big you make your ego, it won't be big enough to satisfy you. Because deep down, you want...*infinity*. You want life without limits. You want the good without limits. You want happiness without limits. And you can never make your ego big enough to hold all that.

Finitum capax infiniti – the finite is capable of the infinite – but only through God's power and love. "Only God can expand the finite to infinity without shattering it."[33] God *wants* to make you "capable of the infinite" – capable of sharing in his infinite life and love. But because God is love, God first waits on your consent and cooperation. God leaves it up to you whether to say Yes or No to being part of something *much* bigger than yourself – *infinitely* bigger. God leaves it up to you to decide whether you are willing to poke some holes in the walls of your fortress ego so that the divine love can flow into you and through you and from you out to others. God leaves it up to you to decide whether you are willing

to take that first, frightening step out of the "safe space" of your
ego and into the infinite spaces of divinity.

36.

Ecstasy through *Ekstasis*

We all want to be happy. As Saint Thomas Aquinas pointed out, we cannot *not* want to be happy. We're not only hard-wired for God. We're hard-wired for happiness. Those turn out to be two ways of saying the same thing.

And actually, we don't want to be merely "happy"; we want *ultimate* happiness; we want the *fullness* of happiness; we want to be as happy as we could possibly be; we want to be *bursting* with happiness; we want to be *ecstatic*. In a fascinating bit of etymology, the derivation of our words "ecstasy" and "ecstatic" actually points us toward the path that leads to ecstasy. "Ecstasy" and "ecstatic" are derived from a Greek word, *ekstasis*, which literally means "to stand outside of oneself". [34] One meaning of "ecstasy" is to be transported beyond oneself in an extreme state of happiness. Well, it turns out that ultimate happiness, the ultimate "ecstasy", results from *ekstasis*, from deliberately stepping outside of one's ego in love, from allowing oneself to be transported out of one's own ego in love toward God and other human beings. Only the path of *ekstasis* leads to true ecstasy.

37.

Aim for Eccentricity

One of our goals in this life should be to become eccentric.
No, not in the sense of "odd" or "peculiar", but in the literal sense
of "ec-centric": having our center *outside ourselves*[35]: first and
foremost in God; secondarily, in our fellow human beings, in the
communio sanctorum. We need to re-center our lives, moving the
focus from ourselves to a focus on God and neighbor.

But on second thought, in today's society, having our center
outside of our own ego *does* make us "eccentric", in the sense of
"odd" or "peculiar", at least in the eyes of many people. But who
cares? *We* know that ultimate fulfillment can't be found within
our own egos. Where's *your* center?

38.

For-ness

"Christ as the man to come is not man for himself but essentially man for others; it is precisely his complete openness that makes him the man of the future. The man for himself, who wants to stand only in himself, is then the man of the past whom we must leave behind us in order to stride forward. In other words, this means that the future of man lies in 'being for'."
Joseph Ratzinger (Pope Emeritus Benedict XVI)[36]

The future of mankind lies in "being for others" rather than "being for oneself". Our individual futures lie in "being for others" rather than "being for oneself". Why have so many of us failed to learn this from Jesus? We've all seen what "being for ourselves" tends to get us: selfish ambition, greed, hardness of heart, broken marriages, broken relationships, enmity, warfare...the list of evils goes on and on. Peace will never come from being exclusively for ourselves.

God calls us to choose to "be for others" in love as the three Persons of the Trinity are "for one another" and "for us". By taking on human flesh and exemplifying how we are called to be "for God" and "for neighbor", Jesus serves as the archetype for us of "being for others". Jesus shows us how being "for others" frees us from the prison of egoism and enables us to enter into the divine freedom, which is the freedom of being for others. We are called to imitate Christ's "'forness'"[37], to enter into and dwell within his "forness". But how do we do that? How can we transcend our ego-centrism and choose to live for God and neighbor? Only by opening ourselves up to allow God to dwell within us, to allow God to act through us, to allow the divine "forness" to flow through us. The more completely we enter into God's form of being-for-one-another, the more completely God can use our lives to benefit others.[38]

Although such a radical renunciation of self-interest can be extremely difficult (even with God's help), the results of transcending one's selfish desires will be far more rewarding than the results of living entirely for oneself. Being for others is "the pure opposite of the boredom of an exitless being-for-oneself." Being for others is a "being-above-and-beyond-oneself, with all the surprises and adventures that such an excursion promises."[39]

In yet another divine paradox, "being for others" turns out to be "being for ourselves", too. Renouncing our self-interest turns out to be in our best self-interest. Strive to be "for others". Strive to be "above-and-beyond-yourself".

39.

Learning How to Die

Life is about learning how to die. More specifically, life is about learning how to die *to self*. As Michel de Montaigne, the French essayist, put it, "He who would teach men to die would teach them to live."[40] Until you have learned how to die, you haven't really learned how to live. Until you have learned how to die, you haven't really learned how to love. To learn how to love is to learn how to die. Genuine love requires dying to self, sooner or later. There's no way around it. If to love is to give the gift of self, then to love is to die a little bit (or sometimes a lot), to die to the part of your self that you give away to the beloved. But by dying in this way, we actually become more fully *alive*, because by dying to self for the sake of another, we enter more fully into the divine life of God, who is Life itself.

So what does "to die to self" mean? It means to die to your *false* self, the self that wants to make itself into God, the self that wants to take the place of God. It means to die to anything that tempts you to center your life on yourself rather than on God and neighbor. It means to die to anything that closes you off from the flow of the divine love. It means to die to anything that blocks or impedes your ability to let that love flow through you to others.

We Catholics are taught to mark ourselves with the sign of the cross on a regular basis. We usually mark ourselves with the sign of the cross at the beginning and end of prayer. We also typically mark ourselves as we enter and leave a Church, dipping our fingertips into the holy water fonts at the entrances and exits of the Church or into the baptismal font prior to making the sign of the cross. We may make the sign of the cross again as we enter and leave a pew in the Church. We make the sign of the cross when the priest blesses us during the concluding rite of the Mass. Like the sacraments, and like other sacramentals, marking ourselves with the sign of the cross has many layers of meaning. Marking ourselves with the sign of the cross is meant to remind us that Jesus died on the cross for us. It reminds us of our baptism, the moment of our incorporation into the Body of Christ. (The use of holy water to sign ourselves makes this connection more vivid.) It is therefore a reminder to ourselves, and a sign to others, that we *belong* to Christ. But perhaps the deepest layer of meaning of marking ourselves with the sign of the cross is as a reminder, and a renewed commitment, to live our lives as Jesus lived his earthly life: in self-sacrificial love for God and neighbor. It is a reminder that we are to be "co-sacrificed" with Christ.[41] It is a reminder that we are called to allow ourselves to be crucified with Christ on the cross of Love (Galatians 2:20).

Most of us are not called to literal martyrdom, but *all* of us are called to die to self in order to live for others. We are all called to live *cruciform* lives, lives lived in the shape of the cross. But the really Good News is that after the cross, comes Resurrection. What shape is your life in?

40.

The Fire of Renunciation

"[L]ove makes us free if it is selfless, and it is selfless if it is ready
to sacrifice pleasure, advantage and independence for the sake
of the beloved. And since no earthly love is initially perfect, it
must go through these purifications. Moments and times must
come when love is tested through sacrifice, when it becomes
clear whether the enthusiasm of the first encounter was love at
all, when the naïve first love – if it really was love – is refined
and deepened in the fire of renunciation."

Hans Urs von Balthasar[42]

To surrender oneself to others in love; to "pour oneself out" in
the gift of self; to enter deeply into the movements of receptivity
and donativity; to open oneself to love and thus to the vulnerabil-
ity and the pain that love can bring; to choose to "be for others"
rather than to "be for oneself"; to empty oneself of the egocentric
concerns and preoccupations that can get in the way of love; to
venture out of the familiar confines of one's ego in love toward
God and neighbor: all of these require *sacrifice*. Sacrifice is an in-
dispensable component of genuine love.

If we are honest with ourselves, we must admit that we realize
that genuine love sometimes requires sacrifice, but we often seek
the joy of love without being willing to make the requisite sacrifices. Such "love" is illusory. Sooner or later, its shallowness, its ego-

centrism, will come to light. We sometimes flee from the pain of sacrifice, but in doing so, we also preclude ourselves from experiencing the rewards and pleasures of genuine self-giving love.

Sacrifice can burn, but it burns with a *purifying* flame, the flame of the divine Refiner. Sacrifice hones our love, polishes our love, *perfects* our love. Sacrifice incinerates the protective walls we've built around our egos. Sacrifice burns away the dross of our selfishness. Sacrifice cleanses us, purifies us. Sacrifice molds us into God's bright image of us. Sacrifice makes us holy (*sacrum facere*). Sacrifice makes us more Christ-like. Sacrifice makes us more like God.

41.

Fluid in the Flowing Spirit

"Love that cannot suffer is not worthy of that name."
St. Clare of Assisi

In this earthly life, love and suffering are intimately connected: if you love, sooner or later, you will suffer. The person you love may reject you. The person you love may abandon you. You may suffer as your beloved (for example, a child now grown to adulthood) makes life choices that divert them from the path of their ultimate good, from the path of Love. Your beloved may die.

To love is to make oneself vulnerable, to open oneself up to the possibility of suffering. Should one then choose *not* to love, in an attempt to avoid the suffering that can accompany love? Absolutely not. As the old saying goes, "Better to have loved and lost than never to have loved at all."

But love and suffering are linked in even deeper, more significant ways. Suffering, like sacrifice, is one of the ways that love can prove its genuineness. Suffering on behalf of another person, perhaps even to the point of dying for the sake of that other person, expresses the depth of one's love like no other expression of love could. When this is understood, both the lover and the beloved can rejoice in that suffering: not because they value suffering for suffering's sake, but because the suffering is undergone out of love and is therefore profoundly meaningful and beautiful.

The depth and the ultimacy of a love that is willing to suffer, even die, for the sake of the beloved is one of the innumerable layers of meaning that underlie Jesus' suffering and death on the cross for us. Just as we are called to share in Jesus' self-sacrificial love for the sake of others, we are also called to share in Jesus' *suffering* for the sake of others. Why? Because suffering, when undergone in the spirit of love, *transforms* us. Suffering for the sake of others, like sacrifices made for the sake of others, makes us more like Jesus. Suffering for the sake of others transforms us more fully into a member of the Body of Christ. Suffering undergone for the sake of love chips away at our stony hearts, sculpting and chiseling them into loving hearts. Suffering undergone for the sake of love softens us, even *liquefies* us, so that we can enter more deeply into the divine flow of love. As Balthasar so beautifully expressed it, "Suffering makes us more fluid in the flowing Spirit, makes us flow into the eternally circulating stream of divine love."[43]

Suffering undergone for the sake of love softens our stony hearts and turns them into hearts of flesh (Ezekiel 36:26). Many of us are willing to spend long hours at the gym in the quest for a sculpted, chiseled body. Sculpted, chiseled bodies can be beautiful, to be sure, but isn't it even more important to have a sculpted, chiseled *soul*? Be willing to suffer for the sake of love.

42.

The Alchemy of Love

Yes, we are called to be willing to suffer for the sake of love. But we are also called to *transform* our suffering *into* love. How could such a thing be possible? How can suffering be converted into love? Only through the alchemy of the divine love.[44]

God will transform our suffering into love that can be distributed to someone in need in the *communio sanctorum* if we ask God to do so. The key here is *intention*: we have to *intend* that our suffering redound to the benefit of someone else; we have to *will* that benefit; we have to *dedicate* our suffering to someone else in a spirit of love. We can unite our suffering to the suffering Jesus underwent on our behalf, for the redemption of the world. When we do that, God takes the love that underlies that dedication and distributes that love to someone who is most in need of that love. As part of your prayer, you might name a specific person to whom you are dedicating your suffering and to whom you wish the divine love and help to flow at this time. Or, you could dedicate your suffering to benefit whomever *God* chooses, the person (or persons) most in need of love and help anywhere in space and time.

This is what Catholics mean when they counsel each other to "offer up" their suffering. As a child, I didn't understand this concept. What good could it do to "offer up" one's suffering to God?

No one had ever explained to me the *intention* behind the offering up of suffering, nor its connection to the communion of saints. Once I did come to understand this spiritual practice, I was struck by its profundity. God gives us the opportunity to turn our suffering into something beautiful, something loving. Our suffering need not be meaningless or pointless. Our suffering can benefit others, if only we choose to endure that suffering in a spirit of love.

"Offering up" our suffering benefits *us*, too, in another one of those beautiful, divine paradoxes. At the simplest level, our suffering can actually become more *tolerable* when it is placed in the service of others. But at a deeper level, "offering it up" can be another step in our transformation into God's bright image of us, chiseling at least a few more chips off our stony hearts.

43.

Empty, but Full

Some of us are too full of ourselves. We're so full of ourselves that there is little, if any, space left for love. To genuinely give and receive the gift of self in love, we have to make some space within ourselves. We have to purge ourselves of all the accumulated baggage that gets in the way of selfless love. This is not easy for us. Most of us are "hoarders" in this regard: we want to cling to all those things that prop up our ego, all those defenses that we have so carefully constructed over the years to shield ourselves from psychological pain, all those walls that we've built up to protect ourselves from other people, from the world, from *God*. Much of it, if not all of it, will have to go. We have to *empty* ourselves in order to make space for love. We have to empty ourselves to make room for the Other/other.

God is the fullness of Being, but in God there is also *emptiness* – the emptiness that makes space for love, the emptiness that makes space for the other within oneself. God the Father does not cling selfishly to his divine attributes, but rather empties himself of all of those attributes in order to hand them over in love to the Son, so that the Son might share fully in his divinity. The Son, in return, does not cling to the gift of self given to him by the Father, but rather completely empties himself in order to reciprocate the Father's gift with his own total gift of self. The Holy Spirit joins in this joyful self-emptying for the sake of love. Emptiness, at least in this regard, turns out to be divine. Our God is a self-emptying God, a God who pours himself out in love. God emptied himself out in creating the cosmos, granting us not only a share in Being, but also the freedom to mess it all up (we've done a pretty good job of that). The Son of God emptied himself of his divinity in taking on our flesh (Philippians 2:5-8) in order to clean up the mess we had made.[45]

There is a Greek word that theologians often use to describe this emptying of oneself for the sake of love: *kenosis*. Because we are called to share in God's divinity, we, too, must join in the divine kenosis, the divine self-emptying. We are called to empty ourselves for the sake of love. For us, the path to fulfillment, the path to *fullness*, must first pass through emptiness. Fullness is attained only by first emptying oneself out. But when you empty yourself out for the sake of love, you will then find yourself filled with a new fullness, a more satisfying fullness, a more joyful fullness. Empty, but full.[46]

PART V

THE MANY FACES OF LOVE

44.

The Primordial Spring

Natural springs are fascinating phenomena. Water continuously wells up from the ground or flows out of a hillside, gratuitously offering its refreshing and life-sustaining qualities, gratuitously offering *itself*, to any thirsty creatures, human or otherwise, that come across it. God is a perpetually flowing spring of life and love, forever giving the divine life away, forever giving *himself* away, to anyone willing to accept the gift.

We're all sustained by the divine Spring, whether we choose to acknowledge that fact or not. We're all sustained in existence, every moment of our lives, by the divine life and love coursing through us. We all drink continuously from the divine Spring – some of us without even realizing it. But God offers us *more* – far more. God doesn't want us merely to drink from the divine Spring of his life and love; God wants us to take great, heaping mouthfuls. God wants to slake our thirst more fully, more deeply than any earthly water ever has or ever could. God doesn't just want us to have life; God wants us to have life *abundantly* (John 10:10). God wants us to share in his *divine* life. God wants to *fill us up* with the divine life and love. And then God wants us to fill our canteens, our water jugs, and whatever else we can round up so that we can carry the life-giving spring water to others, including some people who may not realize what (or actually, *whom*) they're thirsty for, and some people who may not even realize that they're thirsty at all.

Love has many faces. There is the love that one has for one's spouse. There is the love that one has for one's children. There is the love that one has for one's friends. There is the love that one has for oneself. And so on. But ideally, all of these various types of love flow from the ultimate love, the divine love, and are fed and nourished by that love. We love others (and ourselves!) best when our love draws its sustenance, its vitality, its strength, its energy from the divine love. We love best when we drink deeply from the primordial Spring, the primordial Source of all love. We love best when we allow ourselves to be a conduit, a channel for the life-giving water of the Primordial Spring (John 7:37-38).

45.

Open Heart of God, Open Heart of the World

Yes, love has many faces. But the ultimate face of love is...Jesus Christ. Jesus Christ is the ultimate face of love, because Jesus Christ is the visible face of the invisible God who *is* love (Col 1:15). Jesus came to us to reveal the nature of true love to us, the nature of the *divine* love. And what does the divine love look like? An open heart.

Jesus is the heart of God, fully opened up to the world. Opened up to give and receive the gift of self in love, which is the very essence of love. Opened up in the Incarnation, so that God and humanity (and all of creation, through humanity) might be united forever in the person of Jesus. Opened up on the Cross in the ultimate act of self-sacrificial love, so that the entire cosmos might enter into the divine heart and dwell there forever.

Jesus is also the heart of the world, fully opened up to God.[47] As a human being, as one of us, Jesus did what all of us were made for, but none of us manages to do completely[48]: Jesus fully opened himself up to God and his fellow human beings in love. Jesus fully opened himself up to give and receive the gift of self. Jesus fully opened himself to the will of God (which is always love), and to the carrying out of that will in his life. Jesus, as the open heart of the world, did what we couldn't (or, better said, *wouldn't*) do: hand ourselves completely over to God and to our fellow human beings in the loving gift of self. And by doing so, Jesus blazed a trail for us into the very heart of God. Now it's up to us whether we're willing to follow him on that trail or not. But following Jesus will require opening our hearts up to God and neighbor like he did.

46.

Virtus est Ordo Amoris

Saint Augustine wrote that "*Virtus est ordo amoris*" – virtue is the ordering of one's loves. He was right about that, as he was about many things. But we could also say "*Beatitudo est ordo amoris*" – *happiness* is the ordering of one's loves. And we could also say "*Libertas est ordo amoris*" – *freedom* is the ordering of one's loves. And we could also say "*Significatio est ordo amoris*" – *meaning* is the ordering of one's loves. And we could also say "*Pax est ordo amoris*" – peace is the ordering of one's loves. All of the most important aspects of life, the things that matter the most in the end, depend on the correct ordering of one's loves. When you order your loves correctly, all the disparate and fragmented pieces of life tend to fall into place.

Which begs the question: What is the correct way to order one's loves? In one of his most important teachings, Jesus told us how to order our loves: "You shall love the Lord your God with all your heart, and with all your soul, and with all your mind. This is the great and first commandment. And a second is like it, You shall love your neighbor as yourself." (Mt 22:37-39). But Jesus didn't just *tell* us how to order our loves; he also *showed* us how to order our loves by the way he ordered them in his own earthly life. Jesus unquestionably put God first in his life. The Gospels tell us that Jesus regularly retreated from others to pray to God. Jesus stated, several times, that he sought not to do his own will, but the will of God the Father (e.g., Jn 4:34, 5:30, 6:38), including accepting death on a cross (Mt 26:39, 42). Jesus' love for others then flowed from his love for God the Father. Jesus took time, even when he was exhausted, or hungry, or otherwise occupied, to give people his attention, to listen to them, to teach them, to feed them, to heal them.

Most of us have heard the two greatest commandments, but how well are we living them out? Does God *really* come first in our lives? Do we really love God with *all* of our heart, soul, and mind? Or is our love for God, at best, *half*-hearted and lukewarm? So many times, God is an afterthought for us (if we think of God at all): someone we turn to only when we are in desperate straits: during a natural disaster, when we are diagnosed with a serious illness, when we find ourselves in a financial crisis, etc. And what about loving our neighbor as ourselves? How are we doing on the second greatest commandment? It's hard (scratch that; it's *impossible*) to do our best on the second commandment if we're not living out the first commandment. There are reasons why loving God comes first.

And what about the mistake (better said, the *sin*) of putting other loves above either the love of God or the love of neighbor? Love of money, anyone? Love of pleasure? Love of status? Love of power? Disordered loves lead to disordered lives.

47.

Non nisi Te, Domine

Saint Thomas Aquinas, near the end of his life, was praying in a chapel when Jesus spoke to him from the crucifix hanging on the wall. "You have written well of me, Thomas! What do you desire?" And what was Thomas's reply to this rather startling question? "*Non nisi Te, Domine*" – "Nothing but you, Lord". In asking only for the Lord, Thomas knew he was actually asking for *everything*.[49] God, as the Infinite Good, contains all that is good. If you have God, you have everything. If you have God, you have ultimate happiness, freedom, meaning, and peace. If you love God with all your heart, soul, and mind, everything else falls into place, including the ordering of the rest of your loves.

If God spoke directly to you and offered to grant you any request, what would you ask for?

48.

Non nisi Te, Fili

What if God spoke directly to you, but instead of offering to grant *you* a request, he asked you to grant *him* a request? What do you think God would ask you for?

Actually, God's request to each and every one of us is exactly the same: "*Non nisi te, fili*" – "Nothing but you, my child". God wants you, your heart, your self. God offers you himself, and God asks for one thing in return: *your* self.

Aquinas' reply to Jesus of "*Non nisi te, Domini*" was a profound one, on many levels. For one thing, his response showed that he fully realized what (or rather, *who*) the highest Good was, and that he knew to ask for that highest good rather than any lesser goods like wealth, power, a long life, etc. But more importantly, Aquinas' reply showed that he had gained insight into the heart (literally and figuratively) of the relationship that God seeks with each and every human being: the mutual exchange of the gift of self in love.

Of course, God doesn't *need* our love. God is perfect in himself and has no "need" of our love, in the sense of there being a lack or an imperfection in God's state of being that only the love of human beings can address. Nonetheless, God freely chooses to *want* our love, to *desire* our love, because he wants to draw all of us into the sheer bliss of the eternal circulation of the divine love.

Yes, our hearts are definitely restless until they rest in God. But God, out of love, has chosen to allow *his* heart to be restless until he rests in us, and we rest in him.[50] *Non nisi te, fili.*

49.

Commanded to Love?

But if God doesn't *need* our love, why does he *command* us to love him? Why does he *command* us to surrender our heart, our soul, our mind to him?

Some people think human beings can't really be *commanded* to love. Love is something you either feel for someone, or you don't, they say. Their mistake lies in thinking of love as primarily a *feeling*. If love were primarily a feeling, these people would be correct: we can't be commanded to feel a certain way, because feelings tend (at least initially) to well up from the more primitive parts of our brain, outside of our conscious control.[51] But love is not primarily a feeling. Love is, first and foremost, a matter of the *will*, as we reflected upon earlier. We *choose* whether to open ourselves up to give and receive the gift of self in love. We *choose* whether or not to look for the good in other people and whether or not to approve of that good. We *choose* whether or not to will the good of others. We *choose* whether or not to take action to help bring about the good of others. We *choose* whether or not to strive for unity and peace with others. Because love is more a function of our will than of our emotions, love *can* be commanded, just as any other aspect of our will can potentially be commanded.

But the question remains: why does God *command* us to love him if he doesn't really need our love? Because *we* need that love. We *need* to love God, because that's what we were made for. We need to love God because our ultimate fulfillment lies in doing so. We desire, we want, we will, that which we perceive to be good. But in the end, only the Infinite Good can satisfy our desire, because our desire for the good is infinite. We need to love the Infinite Good because only the Infinite Good can fill the infinite void in our hearts.

God commands us to love him because he loves us, and he wills our ultimate good, just as we command our children to do or not do certain things because we love them and we will *their* ultimate good (Eat healthy foods! Brush your teeth! Do your best at school! Don't use illegal drugs!). God commands us to love him because out ultimate good lies in doing so. Our ultimate good lies in sharing in the *Infinite* Good, sharing in God's divine life and love forever. Nothing short of that can satisfy us. And nothing short of loving the divine Love can get us there.

50.

Learning How to Die II

Life is about learning how to die to self, about learning how to sacrifice our own desires at times so that we can love God and neighbor more deeply, as we discussed earlier. But life is also about learning how to die in another sense. Life is about learning how to die *into the arms of God*, learning how to surrender ourselves to God, learning how to hand ourselves *completely* over in love to the God who loves us. That's what God asks for in the "greatest commandment". That's what God wants from us, ultimately: for us to return, willingly, and in love, the gift of our lives that he gave to us willingly, and in love, so that he can transport us completely into his own divine life.

During our earthly life, we should be striving to learn how to make that surrender. For most of us, our surrender to God is, at best, sporadic and partial, but that's still better than a complete refusal to surrender. The more we strive to surrender our lives to God, to hand our lives over to God in love, the more prepared we will be for our eventual physical death, when we *have* to hand our lives over to God. Far better to do so willingly than unwillingly. Our death can be a paroxysm of anxiety, fear, bitterness, etc., or it can be a peaceful surrender to our long-awaited fulfillment, a peaceful surrender into the arms of God.

In Jesus Christ, God surrendered himself completely to us. On the Cross, Jesus' arms are completely extended, open and empty, in a classic gesture of self-surrender. They are also extended in a gesture of embrace. In Jesus Christ, God opens his arms to embrace each and every one of us. God's hope is that we will surrender ourselves into the divine embrace.

51.

Loving Love for Love's Sake

Because we are *creatura*, because we are creatures entirely dependent on God for our very existence, much less our ultimate fulfillment, most of our love for God will always flow from our neediness.[52] But ideally, we eventually get to the point where we love God because God is *good*, not just because we need God and we need everything God gives us. Ideally, our love for God progresses from a love that is primarily self-focused (*eros*, in which we love God because of the ways in which God fulfills our needs) to one that is selfless (*caritas*, in which we love God for God's own sake, or, in other words, love the absolute Good *because* of his goodness and not just because of the good things we receive from him). Ideally, one eventually gets to the point where one loves the Good because it's good to love the Good, not just because it's in one's best interest to do so. Ideally, one eventually gets to the point where one loves Love for Love's sake, simply because Love is good, and Love is beautiful, and Love is true.

Most, if not all, of the canonized saints managed to get to that point before they died. We should strive for that as well. Strive to love Love for Love's sake. But paradoxically, even then, when we're striving to do something completely selfless, to love God simply because God is good and for no other reason, God *still* gives us something good out of it for ourselves. It turns out that it feels *good* to love Love for Love's sake. It feels *beautiful* to love Love for Love's sake. It feels *right* to love Love for Love's sake. Because it is. And because you're right where you were meant to be, right where you were *born* to be: loving the highest Good, possessing the highest Good, sharing in the highest Good.

52.

The Apple of My I

The second greatest commandment, "Love your neighbor as yourself" *assumes* that we love ourselves; but do we? Do we *genuinely* love ourselves? Because if we don't, it's going to be difficult (actually, *impossible*), to love God and neighbor as deeply as we otherwise could.[53] Which means it's going to be impossible for us to be truly happy. But if love is the gift of self, what could it possibly mean to love oneself? How can I give the gift of myself to myself? Well, in the case of self-love, it's more useful to think in terms of the *elements* of self-gift.

Are we able to see, and approve of, the good in ourselves? Many of us struggle with this, sometimes because of a lack of love and affirmation from those who should have loved us the most (our parents, our spouse, etc.), sometimes because we focus excessively on our faults and shortcomings, to the point that it blinds us to the good in ourselves. In what, *ultimately*, does your goodness consist? In how much money you make? In the accomplishments you've achieved in your career? In the power you wield on your job? In the status you've achieved in society? In your good looks? In your radiant personality? No, none of those, of course. Ultimately, your goodness consists in the fact that God loves you, that God willed you into existence and continues to sustain you in existence, that God judges you to be good. You're here because God willed *you* specifically. Any one of an infinite number of other people could have taken your place, but God chose *you*. And that's true of every other person who exists as well. This is the foundation for our doctrine of individual rights: every single human being has value and rights and dignity because God has endowed them with such. When God looked at his creation and proclaimed it very good (Genesis 1:31), he was including you in that assessment, because he foresaw your existence. As we have discussed, there's a unique place reserved just for you in the Body of Christ. You're here for a reason, a unique mission of love within that Body. All of that is what makes you (and every other human being) good.

What about willing your own good? How are you doing on that? Well, actually, we cannot *not* will our own good.[54] We automatically seek the good, because we were built to seek the good. The trouble is, we sometimes make mistakes in choosing what we *think* would be good for us. Are our lives oriented toward the Infinite Good?

Are we acting in a way that will help bring about our good, especially our *ultimate* good? Are we living our lives in a way that will lead us to our ultimate good – *ut in Deo sit* – that we may be in God?

And finally, are we at peace with ourselves? Do we feel whole? Or do we feel fragmented, disjointed? Many of us seek constant distraction (whether it be through sheer busy-ness, or by filling our spare time with social media, the internet, TV, etc.) in order to avoid thinking about the "big issues" in life: where we're at in our relationship with God, how we've been living our lives, how we feel about ourselves, etc. Being at peace with ourselves flows from being at peace with God. And when we're at peace with God and ourselves, it's much easier to be at peace with others, and to love them more selflessly.

53.

Bodily Things Communicated Spiritually, Spiritual Things Communicated Bodily

Love between the sexes has traditionally been presented as the paradigmatic form of earthly loves, first and foremost because sexual love, in its highest form, so fully combines *eros* (love driven primarily by personal desire) with *agape/caritas* (the selfless love that wills the good of the other and is willing to sacrifice for the other to help bring about their good). Sexual love, at its most genuine, is the earthly love that can most fully embody the gift of self that lies at the heart of love. At its best, sexual love actualizes all four of the elements of self-giving love: seeing and approving of the good in the other; willing their good; taking action to bring about their good; and striving for union and peace with the other. In particular, no other earthly love embodies (literally) the element of *union* between lover and beloved more powerfully than does sexual love. Sexual love is the earthly love where "bodily things are communicated spiritually, and spiritual things are communicated bodily".[55]

At the outset, sexual love is mostly, if not entirely, *eros*: love that is driven by personal desire. I choose this person because they have qualities that I desire, qualities that I find attractive, including the sexual pleasure that they could bring to me. But if love is to survive between the man and woman for the longer term, eros must be transformed by agape, purified by agape, *elevated* by agape.[56] One must learn to love one's spouse *selflessly*: to find the good in them even when you'd rather not (like during or after an argument), to will their good and take action to bring it about even when doing so might require tremendous sacrifices on your part, to strive to find a path back to unity and peace with each other when almost every cell of your body (and theirs!) may be screaming: "Run away from this person!"

To insist that eros needs to be purified and elevated by agape is in no way claiming that the erotic element of sexual love needs to be *replaced* by agape. No, as agape becomes more and more present in the love between husband and wife, the erotic element is *heightened*, rather than diminished. The spiritual gift of self synergizes the physical gift of self, and the physical gift of self synergizes the spiritual gift of self. In a healthy marriage, eros feeds agape, and agape feeds eros.

More than for any other person on earth, you are to will for your spouse that they may be *in God* (*ut in Deo sit*). And more than for any other person on earth, you are to do as much as you possibly can for your spouse to help bring that about. When each spouse does that for the other, their love grows fuller and deeper, and their marriage grows into something beautiful, good, and true.

54.

Boring Sex

Sex without the "complications" of love; maximum sexual pleasure with a minimum of personal involvement and commitment: this is the credo of the "hookup" culture. But is this really anything new? No, not really. There were people who advocated this approach to sex at least as far back as the ancient Greeks, more than two thousand years ago. Plato, in one of his dialogues[57], presents some arguments in favor of viewing sex in this way, but ultimately Plato, through the voice of Socrates, emphatically rejects such an approach to sex.

Unfortunately, some people still seek to separate sex from love. As a society, we have increasingly elevated the importance of sexual pleasure while simultaneously devaluing genuine, self-sacrificial love. Paradoxically, such an approach eventually leads to the devaluing of sex as well. Sex becomes cheap (in more ways than one...), supposedly even "free", with no "strings" or "costs" attached. When something becomes so easily available, it tends to lose much of its value and attractiveness. Sex tends to lose not only the joy that should come with it, but even much, if not all, of the physical pleasure that the sex partners were so desperately seeking.

The "hookup" approach to sex is illusory, as anyone who has tried it, especially over the longer term, tends to learn. The hookup may lead to a transient (*highly* transient) feeling of union with the other person, but that feeling, if it occurred at all, tends to be followed by increased feelings of isolation, disappointment, and frustration. As Josef Pieper points out, "What is really sought, human closeness, overcoming of loneliness, union with another personal being – all that can be had only in real love."[58]

Some critics have claimed that Christianity "spoils" sex by surrounding it with numerous do's and don't's. Nothing could be further from the truth. It's precisely *because* sexual love is potentially so joyful, so powerful, so meaningful, so *consequential*, that it needs to be surrounded by do's and don't's that preserve its inexpressible beauty, truth, and goodness. The most important do's and don't's flow from the selflessness that needs to be an integral component of sexual love if it is to be healthy and life-giving for both the wife and the husband. Christianity actually *exalts* sexual love; see, for example, the book of the Bible called the Song of Solomon (also called the Song of Songs or the Canticle of Canticles). Pope Saint John Paul II gave a series of speeches[59] extolling the profound goodness and beauty and meaningfulness of sex within the context of marital love, in contrast with various schools of thought in the course of human history that have disparaged the human body and human sexuality. It's not Christian teaching about sex that "spoils all the fun"; it's the attempt to separate love from sex that does so. Sooner or later, sex without love tends to become empty, meaningless, and yes, even *boring*.

55.

Seeing the Good in Your Better Half

As time goes by, we get to know our spouse better than any other person in our life. After several years (or months, or days, or hours) of marriage, some of us may begin to lose sight of the good in our spouse, to lose sight of the good that initially attracted us to them. Over time, we start to notice more of our spouse's faults, shortcomings, and weaknesses. (Quick tip: Keep in mind that your spouse is noticing more of your faults, shortcomings, and weaknesses, too....) We are then confronted with a choice: are we going to focus more on the good in our spouse, or on the not-so-good? The choice you make at this crossroad will significantly impact the future of your marriage, and the future quality of your life.

Here's a simple five-step process to help you find and approve the good in your spouse: 1) *look* for the good in your spouse; 2) *focus* on that good; 3) *praise* your spouse for that goodness; 4) *re-focus* on the goodness in your spouse (because your attention will sometimes stray toward the not-so-good in them); 5) *repeat* steps 1 through 4 (for the rest of your life).

At some time in the past, when you were first attracted to your spouse, you got at least a glimpse of God's bright image of them; you saw something special in them – special enough to make you choose to marry them. Resolve to regain that vision of your spouse, if you've lost it, and to keep it in focus always. Because as a married person, one of your missions in life is to help your spouse *become* God's bright image of them, through your love and support and encouragement. And one of the best ways to do that is continually to strive to see and affirm the good in your spouse, and to communicate frequently to them the goodness that you see in them. Always keep your eyes open for the "old" good, the good you saw in your spouse early in your relationship, but also be on the lookout for the "new" good: new facets of your spouse that you had never really noticed before, or at least had not sufficiently appreciated before. Notice the gifts and strengths that your spouse possesses, especially the ones that you do not have (or that you have in lesser amounts), and appreciate what those gifts and strengths bring to your marriage, to your family, and to your life. Maybe your spouse is better organized than you; maybe your spouse brings a sense of hope, optimism, and joy to life that counters your own pessimistic streak and lifts you and your family up; etc.

Remind yourself on a regular basis of the good in your spouse, and of the potential for good in them, especially during times of frustration or conflict in your marriage. Make a habit of reminding yourself of the good in your spouse, like counting your blessings. Praise them for the good you see in them. Build them up, instead of tearing them down. If you feel you absolutely must make a negative or critical comment to your spouse, make sure that you do so in an attempt to be constructive, rather than destructive or hurtful, and make sure that your positive, complimentary comments to your spouse outnumber your negative, critical comments by a ratio of at least five to one. On second thought, better make that ten to one. No, a hundred to one. Actually, maybe it's better to leave out the negative, critical comments altogether....

56.

Superglue

For many of us, marriage is the toughest course we will ever take in the school of love (along with parenting). Marriage and parenting are both lab courses in the school of love that is this life: you learn by doing, and you learn as you go. And so does your spouse.

Which brings us to...forgiveness. A word or two (actually, three) about forgiveness in marriage: just do it.

And actually, a few more words: apologize (sincerely) and ask for forgiveness when you need to be forgiven, too.

Forgiveness is one of the glues that helps hold marriages together and keeps them strong. Forgiveness itself requires tremendous strength and will power – another reason we need to stay continuously plugged in to the divine power Source. It can be very difficult to forgive (especially bigger offenses, obviously) purely under our own power. It can also be very difficult to apologize and ask for forgiveness when we need to do so. Forgiving and asking for forgiveness both become easier to do when you ask for God's help.

Sadly, forgiveness is a foreign concept to many people today. It's a lot easier to bolt from a relationship than it is to stay and work things out. Newsflash: that person's next "love" is going to irk them sooner or later, too. The reality is, we all have to learn how to forgive and how to ask for forgiveness (and not just in marriage) if we're going to have any relationships that last.

A final comment about this topic: God doesn't expect any of us to stay in a relationship where there are repeated episodes of *abusive* behavior. God loves us too much for that. This is one of those times when bolting may be the right thing to do.

57.

Soulcraft

If life is a school of love, becoming a parent automatically elevates you to the status of schoolteacher, whether you feel ready for that role or not. As a parent, you are your child's first introduction to love (and to life and to God and to so many other important things...). No pressure there!

Parenting is, of course, about much more than "raising kids", about much more than managing to get your kids safely to age eighteen (or twenty-one, or twenty-nine, or forty-five, or whenever else they're finally mature enough to take over responsibility for their own lives) – although today, that's quite an accomplishment in and of itself. But actually, parenting is about *soulcraft*. As a parent, you have been entrusted with the tremendous responsibility (but simultaneously, the tremendous privilege and *blessing*) of lovingly forming your child's *soul*. You have been entrusted with the tremendous responsibility of sculpting your child's heart in such a way that you give them the best possible chance of growing into God's bright image of them, of growing into the most loving, Christ-like person they can be.

Some people might object to the language of "forming" and "sculpting": "That's way too controlling. I'd never do that to my kids." Well, those are typically the same people whose kids behave like wildlings, whose kids control them instead of them controlling their kids. That approach to parenting is not likely to end well. The reality is, *every* parent shapes and forms their children, whether they realize it (or admit it) or not. That's one of the reasons why parenting is such an important responsibility. The question is, what kind of people are they shaping their kids into?

What do you want for your kids? If you love them, you will their good, especially their ultimate good. And their ultimate good is that they may be in God, that they may share in the eternal circulation of the divine life and love forever. So your most important job as a parent is to help them get there. You do that, first and foremost, by loving them as best as you possibly can. You do that by teaching them about Love and about love. You do that by teaching them that Love and love are what life is all about, and by teaching them how to love. You do that by teaching them about things like beauty, and goodness, and truth. You do that by teaching them to value these goods and to seek these goods in their lives. You do that by teaching them to savor the beautiful, to be and to do the good, to seek and to speak the truth. You do that by teaching your children to seek the Infinite Good above all else, and to open their hearts and minds to him.

58.

Well Done, Good and Faithful Servant

Loving your children as best as you can requires that you continually strive to see, and approve of, and develop, the good that is in them. Like every other human being, your child was created *imago Dei*: capable of learning to love as God loves. Your job as a parent is to help that image of God that is in them to grow into a full-fledged *likeness* to God. Like every other human being, your child has been created for a unique place within the Body of Christ, a place that no one else can fill. Like every other human being, your child has been given a unique mission of love within the overall mission of Jesus Christ to unite all people in the eternal circulation of love that is the divine life. Like every other human being, your child has been given unique gifts and talents by God to help them fulfill that mission.

By continually focusing on the good in your child, by noticing the unique gifts and talents your child has been given, and by praising those good things in your child, you can help them see those gifts and talents in themselves, and you can help them develop those gift and talents to the fullest. Your goal as a parent should be to set your child on the path that gives them the greatest possible chance of saying Yes to God, of saying Yes to their God-given mission, and of subsequently fulfilling that mission. Your goal as a parent should be to do your absolute best to help your child grow into that person to whom Jesus will say, at the end of their earthly lives, "Well done, good and faithful servant...enter into the joy of your master" (Matthew 25:21, 23). If you manage to do that, you, too, will likely receive that most coveted of all approvals.

59.

Unconditional, but Demanding

As a parent, your love for your children needs to be uncondi-tional, but demanding, too.[60] Hmm. Isn't that a contradiction in terms? Actually, no. If you love your children unconditionally, you will always choose to see the good in them, will their good, take action to bring about their good, and strive for unity/peace with them. But "willing their good", in particular, also requires that you place *demands* upon them. Willing their good means willing that they end up possessing the Infinite Good, and that requires willing that they learn how to love, and that, in turn, re-quires having demands placed upon them to teach them to choose love over self. So our love for our children needs to be both un-conditional *and* demanding.

Actually, this mirrors how God loves us. God loves us uncon-ditionally, but his love for us means that he wills our good, which means that he wills that we might share in his life and love, which requires that we learn how to love, which is why God *commanded* us to love him and love one another. The demands God places on us are literally for our own good, just as the demands we place on our children should be for their own good.

Again, some people these days bristle at the idea of placing *demands* on their kids. They want to be the "cool" parent in their kids' eyes, the laid-back parent who's OK with whatever their kids do. Well, their kids might think they're "cool" in the short run, but not so much when those kids grow up and their lives are a mess because they were never taught about the importance of love, self-discipline, self-sacrifice, civility, or any one of a number of other things that help make life go smoothly.

If we genuinely love our children, we want them to be *good*, not just happy.[61] And that requires placing demands on them. They may sometimes resent those demands, but in the long run, they'll be better off because of those demands, and they'll love you for it – eventually.

60.

Sculptor and Sculptee

As a parent, you're not just a sculptor, forming and shaping your child's heart and soul; you're also a "sculptee": *your* heart and soul are being shaped and formed in the process, as well. Parenting is one of the best opportunities we're given in this life to learn how to love selflessly (marriage is one of the others, as is a vocation to the priesthood or religious life). Parenting, when done right, requires tremendous selflessness and self-sacrifice, but it can also be one of the most joyful, fulfilling, and meaningful things you will ever do. It all depends on what you make of the opportunity. Parenting is like most other activities of any significance in this life: the more you put into it, the more you get out of it. And not just in terms of benefits like finding pride and joy in your children, finding meaning and fulfillment in raising them well, etc. Parenting, if you give yourself over to it, and if you let it, will make you into a better person. As you strive to teach your children how to be good and loving, and as you strive to set a good example for them, *you* will become a better and more loving person, too. And that is, after all, what we're all here for.

61.

Friending and Unfriending

C. S. Lewis lamented what he saw as the "ignoring" of friendship in modern society. He claimed that few of his contemporaries valued friendship because few of them experienced it.[62] That was several decades ago. Today, the problem is less that we *ignore* friendship than that we have *cheapened* friendship. Social media have been significant contributors to this change, especially Facebook, with its language of "friending" and those other, oh-so-revealing, terms: "unfriending" and "defriending". Wow - who knew that starting (or ending!) a "friendship" could be as easy as a computer click? Today, "friend" has been cheapened to the level of mere acquaintance and the willingness to be numbered (literally) among someone else's "social network". For some people today, friendship is more about the *number* of friendships listed on one's social media account than the *quality* of those friendships. As a society, our concept of friendship, and our valuing of friendship, is not "trending" in a good direction, shall we say. Of course, social media aren't to blame for all of our ills. Just most of them.

But seriously, there have been other social changes that have contributed to the decline of genuine friendships for many of us. Increasing geographic and social mobility in recent decades has made it more difficult to maintain friendships with people in regions or social strata that one has "left behind". Increasingly hectic lives also tend to leave less time and energy for the cultivation and maintenance of friendships. Some of us are increasingly unwilling to put forth the effort that is required to keep in touch with friends at anything beyond a superficial level, to overlook or forgive hurts that occur between friends, and all of the other things that help to sustain a genuine friendship. But at least now you can more easily keep all your "friends" updated on how great your life is going without them via social media!

Much of what gets called "friendship" these days isn't genuine friendship. Many of those "friendships" are relationships of *convenience* (to the extent that they are "relationships" at all), connections that might help advance my career at some point or that enhance my self-image (and my public image) by their sheer number on my social media account.

Genuine friendship is a form of love. Genuine friends see the good in each other, will each other's good, are willing to take action to help bring about each other's good, and enjoy spending time with each other, enjoy each other's company. To the extent that our "friendships" lack those elements, they are business contacts, or acquaintances, or something else (which is all fine, of course) – but they're not *friendships*.

Resolve to make the time and effort to cultivate genuine friendships, and perhaps to revive friendships that have become dormant for one reason or another. Your life (and theirs) will be richer for it.

62.

People Facing in the Same Direction

How is genuine friendship different from other types of love? C. S. Lewis referred to friendship as the least "instinctive", "biological", or "necessary" of the various kinds of love. Contrasting friendship with eros or sexual love, he claimed that "Lovers are normally face to face, absorbed in each other; Friends, side by side, absorbed in some common interest. ... [Friends] have in common some insight or interest or even taste...." Lewis focuses on that common interest shared by friends as being in some particular *truth*. On this point, he agrees with Ralph Waldo Emerson, who said that in friendship, "Do you love me?" means "Do you see the same truth?" or at least, "Do you *care about* the same truth?" [63] Lewis and Emerson are right about this in the case of some friendships, but the common interest that serves as the basis of friendship should really be expanded beyond *truth* to include some form of *goodness* or *beauty* that both of the friends perceive (or that *all* of the friends perceive, in the case of friendships involving more than two people). Rather than gazing at each other, friends look outward in the same direction, toward that particular truth, goodness, or beauty that they both (or all) perceive in the world and value highly. When we find a person who shares such an outlook with us, we have found an excellent traveling companion on our journey toward *ultimate* Truth, Goodness, and Beauty, our journey *ad Amorem.*

63.

Closing the Circuit

Of course, the reality is, we don't (and in fact, *can't*) choose every single person whose life path crosses ours to be one of our closest friends, to be one of our closest traveling companions on our journey *ad Amorem*. Our outlooks and our values and our tastes don't mesh with theirs like they mesh with those whom we choose as our closest friends. But those other people (all of them!) are still our "neighbors", still our fellow travelers, and therefore we're still called to love them. Every single human being is a member of the species *homo viator*, and we're here to help each other make it to our intended destination. Each of us is here to help at least one other person along that journey (that's our God-given mission in life), and there are other people who are here to help *us* on that journey. That, too, is part of the beauty of this earthly life.

A closed circuit allows electrical current to flow, but an open circuit blocks the flow of electricity. Jesus Christ has laid down circuits leading from God to each and every person so that the divine energy, the divine love, can flow to them, but those circuits sometimes are left open for us to complete for each other. God wants the divine love to flow to everyone, but sometimes we get to be the switch that closes the circuit for someone who has, knowingly or unknowingly, cut themselves off from God. By following

Jesus' commandment to love our neighbor, we can serve as the switch that closes the circuit that Jesus has laid down, enabling the divine love to flow to that person through us. God can, of course, close the circuit without us, but God prefers to give each of us an important role in the circulation of the divine love, a significant part to play in the divine drama. None of us is merely an "extra" in the drama of life.

64.

Going "Off-Grid"

Recently, there has been a small trend toward striving to live "off-grid", which involves disconnecting from the electrical grid provided by the local utility company as well as from other societal resources and attempting to survive entirely off the food, water, and power that can be obtained from the single plot of land on which one lives.[64] Similarly, there has been a trend in recent years among some Christians to strive to live "off-grid" with regard to the *divine* power supply: being a Christian has come to consist entirely of "working for social justice", with little or no attention given to God, or to the worship of God, any more. Going "off-grid" runs the risk of losing our connection to (and our felt need for) God altogether. Balthasar bluntly notes that dissolving the love of God into the love of neighbor can result in a form of "Christian atheism"[65]: God doesn't seem to step in to fix all the injustices in this messed-up world to our satisfaction, so maybe there is no God after all, and it's entirely up to us to mold the world into our vision of a better place....

The focus on loving one's neighbor through efforts aimed at bringing about greater social justice is highly admirable (and necessary), but the commandment to love God sometimes seems to get lost in the social justice shuffle. Loving one's neighbor is *not* a substitute for loving God. Working for social justice is good, but it's not enough, and it's weaker and less effective if it is not rooted in God's love for us and our love for God. We can't close the circuit of the divine love with our neighbor if we're not wired into the circuit ourselves anymore, if we don't keep ourselves connected to the divine flow of energy and love. The more deeply we're connected to the divine love, the more effectively we can love our neighbor. Our love needs to be *both* vertical and horizontal, extending to both God and neighbor. Again, like Jesus, we're meant to be open on *both* sides. And that requires staying "on-grid": on the *divine* power grid, that is.

65.

Unity and Synergy

By becoming one of us in the Incarnation, by uniting divinity and humanity in himself, Jesus Christ has created a *unity* and a heightened *synergy* between the two greatest commandments of loving God and loving our neighbor. By taking on our human nature, Jesus has united himself with *all* human beings of every place and every time. As a result, *every* encounter we have with another human being is, in this sense, also an encounter with *Jesus*, an encounter with *God*. Think about *that* the next time you feel tempted to treat someone badly....

Our fellow human beings are not just "Christ in disguise"; they are, in fact, a *sacrament* of Christ.[66] A sacrament brings the divine life and the divine presence into our lives.[67] Because Jesus has united himself with every human being, every person we encounter brings Christ's presence to us. Every relationship becomes a "new, original, and surprising" encounter with Christ.[68] That's why Jesus told us, "As you did it to one of the least of these my brethren, you did it to me." (Matthew 25:40). When we love our neighbor, we're loving Jesus, too. And when we love Jesus, we are also, through him, loving all the human beings to whom he united himself – which is everybody.

But we still have to do both. Again, loving our neighbor isn't a substitute for loving God. And loving God isn't a substitute for loving our neighbor. But the two greatest commandments do, through Christ, have a greater synergy now. The two commandments are now connected more intimately and more inextricably than before, precisely because they are united in the one Body of Christ. Love for God and love for our neighbors (all of whom are now current or prospective *members* of that Body) feed back on each other, vivify each other, energize each other, strengthen each other, deepen each other. There is a new flow of energy between these two loves because they have been brought together and unified in the one Body of Christ. Love for God and love for neighbor become one in the heart of that Body, in the arteries and veins of that Body. Only as members of that Body can we share in the eternal circulation of the divine love. As members of that Body, one of our missions is to invite prospective members to join the Body. And loving them is the best and most effective invitation of all.

66.

Unlovable?

Sigmund Freud objected to the call to universal love, to the commandment to love *all* of our fellow human beings, claiming that not all people are lovable. Josef Pieper admits that, at first, Freud's statement seems reasonable; we all know, or have known, some people who don't seem very "lovable". But Pieper goes on to point out that, when you carefully consider the judgment that underlies Freud's view of other people, one begins to realize what a "monstrous assertion" his statement that "not all people are lovable" really is.[69]

Recall that one of the essential elements of loving someone is finding some good in that person, finding a reason to be able to say to them "How good that you exist!" To claim that some people are not lovable is thus to claim that it would be *impossible* for *anyone* to find a reason why it is good that that person exists. Which is essentially equivalent to saying that it would have been better if God had never created that person. Who of us is in a position to pass such a damning judgment on anyone else?[70] Would any of us want another person to pass that judgment on *us*? None of us knows the soul of any other person well enough to pass such a judgment on them, nor is it our place to do so. Only God has the knowledge, and the authority, to pass such a judgment on anyone, and the fact that that person exists is proof that God *wills* them to exist and therefore sees good in them and finds them lovable. God invites us, challenges us, to see all other people through *his* eyes, from the divine point of view. God challenges us to find at least some of the good in other people that God sees in them. If God sees enough good in them to have created them in the first place and to sustain them in existence, then that should be good enough (literally) for us to love them, too.

67.

Taking the Long View

During his earthly life, Jesus made several, shall we say, *chal-lenging* statements. Perhaps his most challenging one was "Love your enemies and pray for those who persecute you...." (Mt 5:44). But then, Jesus was always rather good at "seeing the big picture" and "taking the long view" (and still is, of course...). The rest of us? Often, not so much. For many of us, our gut reaction to Jesus' admonition to love our enemies is something along the lines of "No way! You mean I have to find the good in *them*? You mean I have to will *their* good? You mean I have to be willing to actually do something to help bring about *their* good? You mean I'm sup-posed to strive for unity and peace with *them*?" Yes, yes, yes, and yes. Because *God* does all of those things. All of those things are what the divine love does. All of those things are what the divine love *is*. And the divine love is what we are to *become*.

Actually, that is exactly what Jesus goes on to say in the above passage, (although one does not hear this part of the passage quot-ed quite as often): "Love your enemies and pray for those who persecute you, *so that you may be sons of your Father who is in heaven*; for he makes his sun rise on the evil and on the good, and sends rain on the just and on the unjust." (5:44-45; italics added). Jesus is pointing us toward the reason *why* we should love our "enemies": so that we may be sons and daughters of God. In other words, so that we may become more like God. In other, other words, so that we may become more fit to share in the divine circulation of love. So learning to love our "enemies" turns out to be more about us than about them.

With this exhortation to love our enemies, Jesus is encouraging us to look at the big picture, to take the long view. Granted, neither of those is easy to do when we are angry at an "enemy". Rather than looking at the big picture, we tend to have tunnel vision, zeroing in on exactly what our "enemy" did to us that was so wrong, painful, hurtful, etc. and replaying that image over and over in our minds. Rather than taking the long view, we become immersed, not even in the here and now, but in the *past*, clinging to resentments and grudges over things that happened who knows how long ago. The big picture, and the long view, are that you were born to share in the eternal circulation of love, and so was your "enemy". Enmity at the personal, communal, national, and international level is a huge glob of plaque blocking the flow of the divine love in the world. Nursing enmity keeps us (and "them") from sharing as fully as possible in the divine circulation of love. Just *don't* do it.

68.

How to Get Rid of Your Enemies

You should get rid of your enemies. No, not like that, of course. Get rid of your enemies by no longer *thinking* of them as enemies. Admittedly, easier said than done. But Jesus gives us the key starting point in that same passage from the Gospel of Matthew (5:44), when he exhorts us to "pray for those who persecute you". It starts with prayer. And I'm pretty sure Jesus did not mean to pray for your enemy's untimely end, or for your enemy to "get what they deserve", or anything like that. No, Jesus meant to pray for your enemy's *good*. Ask the Lord to *bless* your enemy. This may be especially difficult to do at first; the words may stick in your throat the first few times you try to pray them. But keep at it. Eventually, the words will come more easily. And more importantly, the words will start coming with some more *intention* on your part – you will start to really *mean* the prayer. That transition occurs because praying for your enemy, even if done very reluctantly at first, begins to change how you *think* and *feel* about them. Prayer begins to change your mind and your heart, if you let it. That's the Holy Spirit working on you. Prayer begins to change your mind and heart if you open them up to the possibility of change, if you open them up to the influence of the Spirit. Prayer opens you up to seeing and approving the good in your "enemy". That person is not just someone put here to make your life more difficult (although they may be that, too – God may have made your life cross paths with this person to give you an opportunity to learn to love more deeply, to love even when it seems nearly impossible to do so). No, that person is more than an obstacle to be overcome; that person is a potential or actual fellow member of the Body of Christ, your intended brother or sister in Christ, who has a unique contribution to make to that Body. But that person may also be struggling mightily to make their way through some rigorous lessons in the school of love, just as we all do at times. Who knows (besides themselves and God) what painful experiences that person has been through that make it difficult for them to be more loving, to be a better person, etc.? Part of your mission in life may be to help this person learn how to love better, by doing everything you can to overcome the "enmity" between you. Get rid of your "enemy" by getting rid of your enmity. Start with prayer.

69.

Be Bigger

The spiritual life is full of paradoxes – profound paradoxes. One such paradox is that the more you humble yourself (sincerely, that is), the greater you actually become (Lk 18:14). Unfortunately, some people have a mistaken conception of humility as involving some version of an extreme put-down of oneself, such as "I'm nothing but a lowly worm." Well, that's not genuine humility. The *Catechism of the Catholic Church* defines humility as "the virtue by which a Christian acknowledges that God is the author of all good. Humility avoids inordinate ambition or pride...."[71] Note the key word "inordinate": To humble oneself is to avoid *inordinate* ambition or pride.

So what does all that have to do with loving your enemies? Loving your enemies – *genuinely* loving them – may very well require that you *humble* yourself, as in letting go of some of your inordinate (one could also say, *unhealthy*) pride. What is one of the biggest factors that maintains enmity between self-perceived enemies? *Pride.* We tell ourselves: "*I'm* not going to be the one to take the first step toward making peace. *They're* the one who should do that. After all, I'm the one who's in the right here." The trouble is, the person on the other side is likely thinking the same thing, and so no one makes a move toward resolving the conflict. Strict justice might require that each person make a move toward the middle, so that you can "meet each other halfway". But often, that doesn't happen, either. Your "enemy" may not be willing to "meet you halfway". So what does that mean? If you're going to end the enmity between you, if you're going to genuinely love your enemy, then you probably have to go *more* than halfway. That's what love does. That's what forgiveness does. That's what mercy does.[72] You're going to have to *humble* yourself; you're going to have to let go of some of the pride that is keeping you from resolving the conflict in order to meet the other person more than halfway. And where does the strength to do that come from? From God, who is "the author of all good". God wills the good. God wills there to be peace, not enmity. Which brings us back to prayer. Ask God for the grace (another word for the divine love and life) to meet the other person more than halfway. Ask God to help you let go of some of your inordinate pride and to replace it with the divine love. Easy to do? Absolutely not. If it were, there would be far less enmity, and far fewer enemies, in this world. The call to love our enemies gives a whole new meaning to the phrase "tough love". To love one's enemies is the toughest of all loves, but *somebody* has to take that first step if there is to be peace in this world.

To express the same approach to resolving enmity in a slightly different way: Be the bigger person in the conflict. (So basically, I'm appealing to your sense of pride to encourage you to let go of inordinate pride....) Take the higher road. Transcend the situation. Transcend the conflict. Transcend your wounded pride. The bigger person, the greater person, is the one who loves more deeply than others, even to the point of loving one's enemies. But being the bigger person sometimes requires that you first make yourself smaller – your pride, that is. Making yourself smaller in this way actually makes you bigger. Humility, which is also known as *poverty* of spirit[73], actually leads to magnanimity – literally, *greatness* of spirit. Magnanimous people meet others more than halfway. Strive to be magnanimous. Strive to be great-spirited, like the Holy Spirit of God, who meets all of us far more than halfway.

PART VI

THE FULFILLMENT OF ALL DESIRE

"Love is the prime gift. Whatever else is freely given to us becomes
a gift only through love."
Josef Pieper, *Faith, Hope, Love*

70.

The Rewards of Love

"All true love is without calculation and nevertheless is instantly given its reward, in fact it can receive its reward only when it is without calculation…. Whoever seeks as the reward of his love only the joy of love will receive the joy of love. But whoever seeks anything else in love except love will lose both love and the joy of love at the same time."
Saint Bernard of Clairvaux[74]

"Love is its own reward" – this is absolutely true. Nothing is more rewarding than love, for love is the essence of the Infinite Good. But the beautiful, amazing, astounding truth is that there are many other rewards that come along with genuine love, as long as we don't love merely *for the sake of* those other goods: a deep, abiding happiness; a profound sense of meaning and purpose in life; true freedom; and lasting peace. Which brings us to a deep, existential truth: The best things in life cannot be attained by seeking them directly; they can only be *given* to us.[75] The old saying that "The best things in life are free" points to the same truth.[76] That saying would be better stated as "The best things in life are *gifts*." The best things in life are gifts because they all flow from love, and love itself is a gift, the prime gift, as Josef Pieper noted. These gifts flow from the giver of all good gifts, who is Love

(Jas 1:17). That's why Jesus told us, "Seek first [God's] kingdom and his righteousness, and all these things shall be yours as well." (Mt 6:33). God's kingdom is a kingdom of love; God's righteousness is the righteousness of love.

Seek Love, and seek to be loving, and all these things (happiness, freedom, peace, and a profound sense of meaning and purpose, just to mention a few) shall be yours as well.

71.

The Pursuit of Happiness

"The pursuit of happiness" – this phrase is, of course, enshrined in the Declaration of Independence, penned by Thomas Jefferson on behalf of the American colonies. It's a beautiful phrase. It's an inspiring phrase. But it is also a phrase that can be, in some sense, *misleading*. Do we all desire happiness? Yes, every one of us. Are we all pursuing happiness? Yes, every one of us. But it turns out that if you pursue happiness *directly*, as your main goal in life, you won't find it – at least not deep, lasting happiness. Not *ultimate* happiness. Ultimate happiness cannot be attained by pursuing it directly, even if most of us spend our entire lives trying. Because ultimate happiness is not an end in itself; ultimate happiness is a *consequence* of something else, a *byproduct* of something else. That "something else" is what we should be pursuing. And that "something else" is Love.

Pursue Love, and ultimate happiness shall be yours as well.

72.

The Happiness of Pursuit (and Possession)

So instead of the pursuit of happiness, one could refer to the happiness of pursuit – the pursuit of Love, that is. And the Good News is, that pursuit isn't as difficult as we might think, because it turns out that Love has actually been pursuing *us*. All we have to do is say Yes to Love, and then strive to do our best to *be* love.

Actually, to be more accurate, one should say that ultimate happiness lies in the *possession* of Love rather than the mere pursuit of Love, because of course we want to possess, not just pursue, Love.

Happiness is not just "feeling good", although that's how many people think of happiness. Happiness is possessing something we judge to be good[77], which then causes us to *feel* good. The good feelings that accompany happiness are a *consequence* of possessing something that is good. And the better the "good" we possess is, the better we feel and the happier we are. But the fact is, our desire for the good is *infinite*: we want as much of the good as we can get, and if there's something else out there that's good but that we don't yet possess, we want that, too. That's why we're so restless in this life: we always want *more*. The finite goods of this life can make us temporarily "happy", but that happiness soon fades and leaves us feeling unsatisfied. We then go looking for something else (or someone else) we think will be good, but eventually that good fails to satisfy us, too. Finite goods, precisely because they are finite, can never finally satisfy our desire for *more*. Only the *Infinite* Good, who is God, can satisfy our desire. We were *made* for the Infinite Good. We were *wired* for the Infinite Good. We were made to *share* in the Infinite Good. We were made to share in the divine life and love of God, and nothing short of divinity will satisfy us.[78] Amazingly, divinity is exactly what God has promised us! God has promised us that, through Jesus Christ, we can become "partakers of the divine nature" (2 Pet 1:4) – participants in the very divinity of God!

But there's *more* (God is infinite, so there's *always* more! Try to wrap your head around that one!). Part of the joy of the life to come will lie in the eternal *pursuit*, the eternal *exploration*, of Love. (We get a small foretaste of this in our pursuit of love and Love in this earthly life.) So actually, to be *totally* accurate, one should really say that ultimate happiness lies in *both* the possession *and* the pursuit of Love. For we will be doing both in the life to come. And *that* will be ultimate happiness. In the life to come, there will always (and I do mean *always*) be more facets of the Good, more facets of Love, more facets of *God*, to discover and explore. Heaven is not a static state; it's a *dynamic* state: the most vital vitality, the liveliest of lives, the very fullness of Life itself – perpetually exploring and enjoying and savoring the Infinite Good, and perpetually sharing the Infinite Good with each other. Sounds Good to me.

73.

The Meaning of the World Is Love

"We have been created to love and be loved."
Saint Teresa of Kolkata

"We are all born for love. It is the principle of existence, and its
only end."
Benjamin Disraeli

Of course, we also want other things besides happiness. We
want our lives to *matter*. We want our lives to make a difference.
We want our lives to have *meaning* and *purpose*. For the last several hundred years (since at least the time of the so-called "En-
lightenment") many people have sought such meaning exclusively
within their finite, transitory lives, denying the possibility of some
transcendent realm or reality that could give a deeper, more lasting meaning to their particular lives, and to human existence in
general. But the fact is, this finite life cannot provide us with the
ultimate meaning and purpose that we desire, for the same reason
that it cannot provide us with the ultimate happiness we desire.
We want our life to have a meaning and a purpose that will *last*.
And not just last for awhile after we die; we want our life to have a
meaning and a purpose that will last *forever*. Our desire for a sense
of meaning and purpose in life is *infinite*, as is our desire for all

the other greatest goods of life: happiness, freedom, peace, beauty, goodness, truth, and life itself. This finite life cannot fully satisfy *any* of our deepest desires, because all of those desires are *for* the Infinite, for the One who is infinite bliss, infinite freedom, infinite peace, infinite beauty, infinite goodness, infinite truth, and infinite life itself, and in whom our lives find their ultimate meaning and purpose. And what is that ultimate meaning and purpose? *Love*, of course. Balthasar got it exactly right: The meaning of the world is love.[79] Love is why you are here. Love is why I am here. Love is why the world, and the entire cosmos, are here. The meaning of life is love, because love is the essence of Life. Love is what life, and Life, are all about. Life is all about the eternal exchange of the gift of self with God and with our fellow human beings. Life is all about the eternal circulation of love.

God wired a desire for lasting meaning and purpose into us because God *made* us for a lasting meaning and purpose: to live forever as an irreplaceable member of the Body of Christ and to fulfill a unique mission of love within that Body, a mission of love within the eternal circulation of love that no one else can fulfill in our place. Our lives take on the permanent, eternal meaning and purpose we so desperately seek only if they are rooted in, and dwell within, the Infinite Good, who is Love, and who is the meaning of it all.

Seek Love, and seek to be loving, and ultimate meaning and purpose in life shall be yours as well.

74.

Mission: Implausible II

In at least four different places, the Gospels record Jesus telling us that if we want to follow him, we must "take up our cross" (Mt 10:38, 16:24; Mk 8:34; Lk 9:23). So apparently this was a rather important part of Jesus' message to us. By "taking up our cross", Jesus is referring, at least in part, to accepting, and doing our best to fulfill, our mission of self-sacrificial love. Whatever your mission might be, it will require self-sacrifice from you, because it is a mission of love, and genuine love requires self-sacrifice, as we have seen.

One of the many intriguing passages in Scripture is Saint Paul's reference to "complet[ing] what is lacking in Christ's afflictions for the sake of his body" (Col 1:24). In that passage, Paul is primarily referring to his own sufferings on behalf of the Body of Christ, but it is clear from the context and from other passages as well that we, too, are called to share in the sufferings of Christ for the sake of the Body (see, for example, Rom 8:17 and Phil 3:10). Paul does not mean that Jesus' suffering on the Cross was somehow insufficient for our redemption; his suffering was totally sufficient for our redemption. Rather, Paul is referring to the fact that God has given each of us the opportunity to *share* in Jesus' sufferings for the sake of love, to share in Jesus' self-sacrifice for the sake of other members of the Body of Christ. Some theologians have gone so far as to refer to us as "co-redeemers" with Christ. God has given each of us the tremendous dignity, and responsibility, of doing something important for the rest of the Body of Christ, of making a meaningful contribution to the building up of that body through the mission of love that has been entrusted to us.

Each of us is called to carry a mere splinter of a cross, compared to what Jesus endured for us. But that splinter still has infinite value and meaning, because that splinter of a cross represents our impact on at least one other member or potential member of the Body of Christ through our life of self-sacrificial love, and that person is of infinite value to God. Through the alchemy of love in the communion of saints, the sacrifices we make and the sufferings we endure on behalf of love can benefit others and make a unique contribution to the Body of Christ.

For most of us, our mission is not going to make us famous, nor is our mission itself going to receive much, if any, publicity. Most saints, and would-be saints, labor in relative anonymity. But God knows what we're doing for love, as do at least some of the people for whom we make loving sacrifices. And that should be enough for us in this life.

Pray to see clearly your mission in life, and pray for the grace to fulfill that mission. That mission is the key to the ultimate meaning and purpose of your life.

75.

Free to Choose the Good

Why is there so much evil and suffering in the world? In a word, *freedom*. We human beings have been given the freedom to choose between good and evil, and sadly, tragically, we often choose the latter. And choosing evil inevitably leads to suffering, sooner or later (often, both sooner *and* later). To choose evil is, by definition, *not* to choose the good, and failure to choose the good is, well, not good. Choose the good, and receive the good; choose against the good, and bad things happen. It's as simple as that. But we often choose against the good anyway.

Which leads some people to ask: Why couldn't God have made us so that we *always* choose the good? Well, if we were made in such a way that we could *only* choose the good, we would not really be making a choice at all. We wouldn't be free, and all of the meaning and drama of this life would be drained away. We would be mere automatons. The drama and the meaningfulness of this life *hinge* on our freedom to choose between good and evil. The path your life takes, and your ultimate destiny, hinge on this choice.

Actually, it isn't only the drama and meaningfulness of life that hinge on freedom. *Love* hinges on freedom. Without freedom, love cannot exist. Love cannot be forced; love cannot be coerced. Love must be freely offered, and freely received. "Love" that is programmed into a robot isn't really love at all. And apparently God judged love to be so good, so valuable, as to be worth the price of evil and suffering that would result from our misuse of our freedom.

Many people today have a distorted concept of freedom. They think of freedom only as the *freedom to choose*. Freedom, to them, means being able to choose whatever they want; freedom means being able to *do* whatever they want. But genuine freedom is more than that. Genuine freedom is freedom to choose *the good*. Don't leave that last part off. People who think freedom consists entirely in the *power to choose* have elevated freedom itself above the *object* of freedom, which is the good, and which is our ultimate goal. For such people, the power to choose becomes more important than *what* they choose.[80] They are gravely mistaken.

Every time we choose good over evil, our freedom grows. The greater the good we choose, the more our freedom grows. If we choose the greatest good, the Infinite Good, our freedom grows infinitely. The greatest good is, of course, Love, and so the greatest freedom lies in choosing Love and love.

76.

Nothing Frees So Deeply As Love

We have been set free by Love. We were set free by Love so that we might be free to choose whether to return to Love. Genuine freedom flows from and toward Love. Our finite freedom finds its ultimate fulfillment only in the infinite freedom of God, whose freedom consists precisely in love, precisely in the gift of self, given and received.[81] When we join in the eternal circulation of love, we share in the infinite freedom of God.

If you refuse to surrender yourself in love to Love, you are not truly free.

If you refuse to give yourself away in love to your fellow human beings, you are not truly free. You will not attain greater freedom by refusing to give yourself away in love; rather, you will find yourself more deeply enslaved to the voracious and insatiable desires of your tyrannical ego.

If you choose to remain within the cramped confines of your ego rather than stepping out of yourself into the infinite spaces of the divine freedom in the *ekstasis* of love, you are not truly free.

If you refuse to open yourself up to receive the self-gift of God and neighbor, you are not truly free.

If you refuse to sacrifice for the sake of love, you are not truly free.

If you refuse to empty yourself on behalf of the beloved in the *kenosis* of love, you are not truly free.

If you refuse to carry out the mission of love with which you have been entrusted, you are not truly free. It is yet another paradoxical spiritual truth that the greatest freedom lies in *serving* rather than in being served.

Ultimate freedom is found only in the self-transcendence required by genuine love. Nothing frees so deeply as love.[82] Seek Love, and seek to be loving, and ultimate freedom shall be yours as well.

77.

He Is Our Peace

To be at peace with others, we need to be at peace with ourselves. And to be at peace with ourselves, we need to be at peace with God, as we reflected upon earlier. Jesus Christ has brought about this peace between us and God (Rom 5:1; Col 1:20). In fact, Jesus hasn't just *brought about* this peace; Jesus *is* our peace. He has made us all one; he has "broken down the dividing wall of hostility" that used to separate us from each other (Eph 2:14-18). Ultimate peace is found only in Jesus Christ. Ultimate peace is found when we unite ourselves to Jesus, when we are joined to his Body and continue to dwell within that Body, *united* with God and *united* with all other members of the Body of Christ. So once again, we find that the fulfillment of one of our deepest desires in life, our desire for *peace*, can only be found in Love. Peace is shattered by division and disharmony; peace is restored when union and unity are reestablished. *Lasting* union and unity can be brought about only through love.

Saint Paul told the Romans that "to set the mind on the Spirit is life and peace" (Rom 8:6). The Holy Spirit of God is the Spirit of Love, so "to set the mind on the Spirit" is to set the mind on the Spirit of Love. Set your mind (and heart) on Love, and you will find life and peace as well.

78.

Peace Is Flowing Like a River

Setting your mind and heart on Love requires that you open your mind to Love as the ultimate reality, and that you surrender your heart to Love. There is a profound peace that comes from surrendering your life to God. Handing your life over to God in love and gratitude feels good; it feels right. You're where you were meant to be. You're *home*. All of your searching, all of your longing, finds fulfillment here: in God, in the Body of Christ. *This* is what you have been searching for, maybe for your whole life. *This* is what you have been longing for. To be at peace with God, to be united with God, to share in the divine life, to be one with Being itself. To be at peace with, and to be united with, your fellow human beings who have also surrendered their hearts and their lives to God.

The peace that flows from handing your life and your heart over to God is the peace that Jesus conferred on his disciples, and it is the peace that he wants to confer on us. It is not just any peace; it is *his* peace; it is the divine peace: "Peace I leave with you; *my* peace I give to you; not as the world gives do I give to you. Let not your hearts be troubled, neither let them be afraid." (John 14:27; italics added). So many of us spend our lives frantically searching for that elusive "something" in the world that will fulfill us, that will bring us happiness and peace: that romantic partner, that luxurious house, that big bank account, that career achievement, etc. Those are all potentially good things, but they're not the *ultimate* good, the infinite good, the only good that will bring us *lasting* happiness and peace: God. Nothing less than God, nothing less than a share in the divine life, will bring us the lasting happiness and peace we seek. Saint Augustine expressed this truth perfectly when he exclaimed, "You have made us for yourself, O Lord, and our hearts are restless until they rest in You."[83]

"Peace" is referred to more than ninety times in the New Testament.[84] Clearly, the Holy Spirit, who inspired the writers of the Bible, wants us to know where true peace is found: only in Jesus Christ; only in surrendering our lives to God in love; only in giving the gift of self to God in loving gratitude for God's loving gift of self to us.

Life is a river, bearing us onward toward the vast ocean of love that is the divine life. We can relax and entrust ourselves to the current of that river, gradually even learning to swim with the current, or we can fight the current and spend our entire lives frantically trying to swim upstream. Life can be a loving surrender into the arms of God, or an ongoing struggle against our intended destiny, forever fleeing from the only destination that will fulfill us and bring us peace. Peace truly is flowing like a river. Go with the flow.

79.

Guide Our Feet into the Way of Peace

The best response to the problems besetting the world today is not a new political or economic or social program. No, the best response to the problems of the world is a spiritual response: a response of selfless love, a response of sacrificial love, a response of love that extends even to one's "enemies". If there is to be peace on earth, the best place to start is at the level of converting individual hearts to be more like the heart of Jesus.[85]

And the first heart to work on converting more fully to the heart of Jesus is...our own. The song entitled "Let There Be Peace on Earth" gets it exactly right when it follows the title line with the line "and let it begin with me." Ultimately, there will be no peace on this earth unless and until individual people, and individual nations, deliberately *choose* peace and *strive* for peace.

Pope Saint Paul VI exhorted us to strive to build a "civilization of love", and Pope Saint John Paul II echoed that call. That civilization will not come about through the pursuit of, and accumulation of, more political or economic power, either by individual people or by individual nations. Rather, the civilization of love will only truly come about when individual people, and individual nations, begin to be willing to substitute the seeming powerlessness of selfless love (which turns out to be *true* power) for the endless pursuit of economic and political power. And *that* will only come about through divine help, through a new outpouring of the Spirit of Love on the world. Pray for that. Pray for peace.

Lord, fill us with your Spirit of love. Fill the world with your Spirit of love. Make our hearts more like yours. Guide our feet into the way of peace (Lk 1:79).

80.

Beauty Is More than Skin Deep

The old saying that "beauty is only skin deep" does, of course, contain a grain of truth. Sometimes someone who appears beautiful on the outside does turn out to be not quite so beautiful (to put it politely) on the inside. But in another sense, beauty (*genuine* beauty) *isn't* only skin deep. Genuine beauty is far *more* than skin deep. Beauty points beyond itself. Beauty is a window onto the transcendent. The beauty of a flower, the beauty of a captivating sunset, and the beauty of an exquisite sculpture or painting all point beyond themselves, to something deeper. Beauty points to the very depths of reality, to the very depths of being itself. Beauty points to…God.

The beautiful object is an *epiphany*, a *theophany*, a revelation of God. The beautiful object is a radiation of the divine love that points to the Lover behind that love, the Beauty behind that beauty. Beauty points to Love, because Love is the source of all beauty and because the ultimate beauty *is* Love. The divine beauty is the beauty of the divine love. After all, what is more beautiful than self-giving, self-sacrificial love, raised to an infinite degree? As the revelation of the divine love, and as God's loving gift of self to all human beings, Jesus Christ is the ultimate icon and model of all beauty.[86] In the words of Fyodor Dostoevsky, "There is really only one positively beautiful figure: Christ."[87]

Our desire for earthly beauty runs deep within us, in part because that desire is a manifestation of our even deeper desire for the *ultimate* Beauty. As C. S. Lewis insightfully observed, "We do not want merely to *see* beauty, though, God knows, even that is bounty enough. We want something else which can hardly be put into words – to be united with the beauty we see, to pass into it, to receive it into ourselves, to bathe in it, to become part of it."[88] Our desire to "be united with", to "pass into", and to "become part of" the beauty we see is a reflection of our deeper desire to be united with, to pass into, and to become part of the ultimate Beauty: the divine life and love.

Seek Love, and seek to be loving, and beauty shall be yours as well.

81.

Awakening Sleeping Beauty

To a large extent, modern society has lost touch with beauty. How many works of "art" produced in the last hundred years or so are truly *beautiful*? How many even deserve the honor of being referred to as a work of *art*? How many truly beautiful paintings have been produced in that period? How many beautiful sculptures? How many beautiful works of literature? How many beautiful movies? How many beautiful television programs?

OK, but is all that really such a big deal? *Yes.* Our loss, as a culture, of much of our awareness of, and genuine appreciation for, beauty has serious implications. When we begin to lose our ability to perceive the truly beautiful, we also begin to lose our ability to perceive that which is good and that which is true, as well. These three aspects of life, these three aspects of *being* itself (beauty, goodness, and truth), are tightly connected with each other, intimately interwoven. Because of those interconnections, one cannot entirely separate them from each other. If you try to separate one of these from the other two, you end up losing all three. Pull hard enough on one thread, and the entire tapestry starts to unravel. When you begin to lose your awareness of, and appreciation for, the beautiful, the good, or the true, you begin to lose touch with much of what enriches life, with much of what makes life worth living.

Our hearts seek beauty; our wills seek the good; our minds seek the truth. These desires are, at least in part, a reflection of our desire for the fullness of *life*, the fullness of *being*. We aren't satisfied with mere survival. We want to *really* live, to be fully *alive*. And to be fully alive, we *need* beauty, goodness, and truth. Philosophers (at least those who know what's good for them) have referred to these three qualities of being as "transcendentals" because they *transcend* the traditional categories into which we tend to divide and classify being. Beauty, goodness, and truth pervade *all* being, pervade all that exists. The entire cosmos is suffused with beauty, goodness, and truth because it flows from the One who *is* Beauty, Goodness, and Truth. Our desire for beauty, goodness, and truth are all, at least in part, manifestations of our deeper desire for *God*.

If we desire beauty, goodness, and truth so much, why have we, as a society, lost touch with them? One major factor has been the increasing popularity of a materialist view of existence, one which says that physical matter is all that exists, and that life is a mere epiphenomenon of blind physical and biochemical processes within that matter. The materialist view denies the existence of a transcendent realm, a realm that transcends, while also incorporating, the physical realm. There are no objective standards of beauty; beauty is purely subjective. There are no objective standards of goodness; either. The good is that which any of us, individually, choose to *designate* as good for ourselves, nothing more. Truth, if it is not denied entirely, tends to be reduced to only those "facts" that can be empirically demonstrated using the scientific method.

One of the many negative consequences of adopting a materialist view of life is that it sucks much of the goodness (yes, *goodness*) out of life. Many materialists end up being extremely cynical about the goodness and the value and the meaning of life, if not outright nihilistic. That is one of the key reasons why our loss of touch with genuine beauty, goodness, and truth has been downright tragic. Beauty, goodness, and truth are pathways to the transcendent. Beauty, goodness, and truth are pathways to love. Beauty, goodness, and truth are pathways to God. If we lose touch with objective beauty, goodness, and truth, we lose our ability to pray, and eventually our ability to love.[89] The latter is not coincidental. Beauty, goodness, and truth, like *all* of the most important and most meaningful aspects of life, are all connected to love and rooted in love, because they all have their source in Love. Love, it turns out, is the fundamental transcendental, the one that undergirds beauty, goodness, and truth.[90] Lose beauty, goodness, or the fullness of truth, and you start to lose love as well.

So if beauty has fallen into a deep sleep in our culture, how do we awaken her? With a kiss, of course. (The same thing goes for Sleeping Goodness and Sleeping Truth). Some of us need to learn (or re-learn) what genuine love is. Some of us need to learn (or re-learn) that love is of paramount importance in life. Some of us need to discover (or rediscover) the God who is Love. When you're *in Love*, you will find yourself surrounded by beauty, goodness, and truth. Love enables us to see beauty, goodness, and truth more clearly, and perceiving beauty, goodness, and truth more clearly better enables us to love.

To get there, some of us need to adopt a more open mind (and heart) to the possible existence of a transcendent realm, a realm which grounds the objectivity of the beautiful, the good, and the true. After all, who is more "open-minded": the person who flat out denies the existence of such a realm, or the person who at least remains open to such a possibility, since neither its existence nor its non-existence can be demonstrated conclusively in this life? In opening oneself up to the possible existence of a transcendent realm, one also opens oneself up to the possibility that there are such things as objective beauty, goodness, and truth.

We need to teach our kids to be open to beauty, goodness, and truth. We need to teach them about the *objective* beauty, goodness, and truth of life. We need to teach them to see, and value, that beauty, goodness, and truth. We need to form and shape their hearts to seek the beautiful, their wills to choose the good, and their minds to seek the truth.

We also need to challenge those who produce works of art and our other cultural artifacts (paintings, sculpture, architecture, movies, TV shows, music, books, etc.) to strive to produce works that express and embody beauty, goodness, and truth.

In the end, for any of us to be able to perceive, and truly *experience*, the beautiful, the good, and the true (and therefore the depths of being to which beauty, goodness, and truth point), we have to choose to *open ourselves up* to beauty, goodness, and truth. No one can do it for us. That's part of our freedom, too.

82.

The Unbearable Goodness of Being

Take time to stop and marvel at the fact that all of this – life, the world, the cosmos, everything that exists – simply *is*. When you really stop to think about it, isn't it amazing/astounding/astonishing/marvelous/wonderful that all of this *is*? None of this, including you and me, *had* to be. And yet, here we are. From the microscopic level to the cosmic level, from the delicate beauty of the smallest flower to the grandeur of the stars in the sky, it's all amazing and beautiful and wonderful and *good*, if we simply open ourselves up to see and appreciate that goodness. Being is good simply because it *is*. Being is good by virtue of its very existence. It's *good* to be. And it's infinitely better to be than not to be, to answer Hamlet's agonized question.

Most of the time, we take everything (and I do mean *everything*) for granted. We take the continued existence of everything around us, and the daily continuation of life itself (especially our own), as a given. Those two words, "granted" and "given", are actually very revealing. We have been *granted* all these things. We have been *given* all these things, including our selves, our very existence. Everything is *gift*. Or, as Saint Thérèse of Lisieux put it, everything is *grace*. Being is good, not only by virtue of its very existence, but also because *being gives itself*. It's astounding that any of this exists at all, but it's even more astounding that everything that exists *gives* itself. That's what being does. It gives itself. Being gives itself to our senses, and thus to our emotions and to our hearts: being is beautiful. Being gives itself to our wills: being is good. Being gives itself to our minds: being is true.[91]

Giving lies at the heart of being, because giving lies at the heart of Being. Giving lies at the heart of Being, because giving lies at the heart of God. Giving isn't just something God does; giving is what God *is,* because God is love and to love is to give. Everything that exists retains a vestige of its Creator.[92] That vestige consists, at least in part, in the fact that all of creation gives itself just as Being gives himself. We human beings are gifted with more than a *vestige* of our Maker. We are made in God's *image* in our ability to choose, freely and consciously, whether we are *willing* to give ourselves in love to God and neighbor, and whether we are *willing* to open ourselves up to receive their gift of self. We are free to choose whether or not we are willing to enter into the "dynamic of the gift"[93], which is the dynamic of divinity and hence the dynamic of Being itself. The more fully we enter into the dynamic of the gift, the more fully we share in Being and therefore the more fully alive we are. The more fully we enter into the dynamic of the gift, the more fully we share in the Good that we so deeply desire.

Seek Love, and seek to be loving, and the good shall be yours as well.

83.

Love Is Truth

When Jesus was being interrogated by Pontius Pilate, the Roman governor of Judea, Jesus told Pilate "For this I was born, and for this I have come into the world, to bear witness to the truth. Every one who is of the truth hears my voice." To this, Pilate cynically retorts, "What is truth?" (John 18:37-38).

Aquinas defined truth as "the equation of thought and thing" – a precise correspondence between our thinking and the thing which we're thinking about. Truth is a statement of the way things *are*, an accurate description of reality. When we say to someone, "Tell me the truth!", we're asking them to tell us the way things *really are*. At an even more profound level, truth is a *revelation*, an unveiling, a disclosure of reality, a disclosure of the nature of *being* itself.[94]

Because our society has largely reduced "truth" to empirically verifiable facts, we have tended to lose touch with these deeper, more important truths: truths about *being* itself; truths about life itself. Why are we here? What is life all about? Is there any ultimate meaning or purpose to life? And so on. And without these truths, our lives are set adrift: empty, aimless, pointless, meaningless.

The truth about being, the truth about life, the truth about the way things are, is...*love*. Love *is* truth. [95] Love is the truth because love is the essence of reality, the essence of Being itself, the essence of *God.*

That's the truth that Jesus came to "bear witness to". But that's not all. Jesus didn't just come to bear witness to the truth; Jesus *is* the Truth (John 14:6). Pilate appears not to have realized it at the time, but he was actually *looking* at Truth and *speaking* with Truth when he was interrogating Jesus. Jesus is the embodiment of Truth, because he is the embodiment of God, who is Truth itself, reality itself, Being itself. Jesus came to reveal to us that self-giving love is the Truth of Being, the *way things are.* Jesus came to open up the path to that Truth for us. Jesus came to be *that* path for us.

Everyone who is "of the truth", everyone who is genuinely open to the truth, wherever the truth may take them, hears the voice of Jesus and heeds it. In contrast, "Whoever does not let love take over excludes himself from the truth...."[96]

Seek Love, and seek to be loving, and truth shall be yours as well.

PART VII

BEING SOMEBODY,
GOING SOMEWHERE

84.

Being Nobody, Going Nowhere

Sadly, tragically, there are people who believe that they are "nobody going nowhere", and at least some of those people would like to convince you that *you're* "nobody going nowhere" too. There's actually a book entitled *Being Nobody, Going Nowhere*[97], a song called *Being No One, Going Nowhere*,[98] and another book with the title *Being No One*. Do I detect a theme here? Here's a passage from the latter book, which was written by a German philosopher named Thomas Metzinger:

"The illusion is irresistible. Behind every face there is a self. We see the signal of consciousness in a gleaming eye and imagine some ethereal space beneath the vault of the skull, lit by shifting patterns of feeling and thought, charged with intention. An essence. But what do we find in that space behind the face, when we look? The brute fact is there is nothing but material substance: flesh and blood and bone and brain...You look down into an open head, watching the brain pulsate, watching the surgeon tug and probe, and you understand with absolute conviction that there is nothing more to it. There's no one there."[99] (Which raises the obvious question: if "There's no one there," to whom was he addressing his book?)

So Metzinger's message to every human being, including you and me, is "You're nothing. You're nobody." We get similar messages from other materialists, insisting, for example, that we human beings are "nothing but a pack of neurons".[100] Is it any wonder that some people, hearing such claims, believe that their life has no meaning or purpose? Is it any wonder that they believe they really *are* nobody going nowhere?

"Being nobody going nowhere" does have some advantages, I suppose. If everybody's a nobody going nowhere, then nobody has to feel responsible, maybe even a little guilty, for failing to become somebody, for failing to do something meaningful with one's life. Plus, if everybody's a nobody going nowhere, then nobody can criticize me for being a slacker, a low achiever, a… well, a *nobody*, because *everybody's* a nobody. If everybody is nobody, then nobody is somebody. Hmmm. Wait a minute. If everybody is nobody, and nobody is somebody, then everybody really is somebody after all![101]

And in fact, they are. Everybody really is somebody. Everybody really is somebody going somewhere, not nobody going nowhere. The question is, where is everybody going?

85.

Being Somebody, Going Somewhere

You are meant to be somebody going somewhere. I'm meant to be somebody going somewhere. Everyone is meant to be somebody going somewhere. Who are we, and where are we meant to be headed? Well, as to the "somebody": we're all somebody because every one of us is made *imago Dei*, in the image and likeness of God, with the capacity to love and with a unique mission of love to fulfill in this life that no one else can fulfill in our place. And as to the "somewhere": we're meant to be headed toward God, toward Love, toward the eternal circulation of love. We're all *homo viator*, on a journey *ad Amorem*.

But it's up to us whether we want to live up to the "somebody" that God has made us to be, and it's up to us whether we want to reach the "somewhere" that God has intended us to be. Our ultimate happiness, and the ultimate meaning of our lives, hinge on the choice we make. That's one of the reasons why our lives *matter*, why each of our lives *matters*. Our eternal destiny hinges on the response we choose to make to Love's offer, to Love's invitation, which is issued to each and every one of us. Choose to be somebody going somewhere instead of nobody going nowhere.

BIBLIOGRAPHY

Aquinas, Thomas. *Summa contra Gentiles.* Vol. 3, *Providence,* translated by V. J. Bourke. Notre Dame, IN: University of Notre Dame Press, 1975.

Augustine of Hippo. *Confessions.* Translated by Vernon J. Bourke. Washington, D.C.: Catholic University of America Press, 1966.

Balthasar, Hans Urs von. *The Christian State of Life.* Translated by Sister Mary Frances McCarthy. San Francisco: Ignatius, 1983.

Balthasar, Hans Urs von. *Credo: Meditations on the Apostles' Creed.* Translated by David Kipp. San Francisco: Ignatius, 1990.

Balthasar, Hans Urs von. *Elucidations.* Translated by John Riches. San Francisco: Ignatius, 1998.

Balthasar, Hans Urs von. *Explorations in Theology.* Translated by Edward T. Oakes. Vol. 4, *Spirit and Institution.* San Francisco: Ignatius, 1995.

Balthasar, Hans Urs von. *Explorations in Theology*. Vol. 5, *Man Is Created*, translated by Adrian Walker. San Francisco: Ignatius, 2014.

Balthasar, Hans Urs von. "The Fathers, the Scholastics, and Ourselves." *Communio: International Catholic Review* XXIV (2) (1997): 347-396.

Balthasar, Hans Urs von. *The Glory of the Lord: A Theological Aesthetics*. Vol. 1, *Seeing the Form*, tranlated by Erasmo Leiva Merikakis. San Francisco: Ignatius. 2009.

Balthasar, Hans Urs von. *The Glory of the Lord: A Theological Aesthetics*. Vol. 2, *Studies in Theological Style: Clerical Styles*, edited by John Riches and translated by Andrew Louth, Francis McDonagh, and Brian McNeil. San Francisco: Ignatius, 1984.

Balthasar, Hans Urs von. *The Glory of the Lord: A Theological Aesthetics*. Vol. 4, *The Realm of Metaphysics in Antiquity*, edited by John Riches and translated by Brian McNeil C.R.V., Andrew Louth, John Saward, Rowan Williams, and Oliver Davies. San Francisco: Ignatius, 1989.

Balthasar, Hans Urs von. *The Glory of the Lord: A Theological Aesthetics*. Vol. 5, *The Realm of Metaphysics in the Modern Age*, edited by Brian McNeil, C.R.V. and John Riches; translated by Oliver Davies, Andrew Louth, Brian McNeil C.R.V., John Saward, and Rowan Williams. San Francisco: Ignatius, 1991.

Balthasar, Hans Urs von. *The Glory of the Lord: A Theological Aesthetics*. Vol. 7, *Theology: The New Covenant*, edited by John Riches; translated by Brian McNeil, C.R.V. San Francisco: Ignatius, 1989.

Balthasar, Hans Urs von. *Heart of the World*, translated by Erasmo S. Leiva. San Francisco: Ignatius, 1979.

Balthasar, Hans Urs von. *In the Fullness of Faith: On the Centrality of the Distinctively Catholic*, translated by Graham Harrison. San Francisco: Ignatius, 1988.

Balthasar, Hans Urs von. *Light of the Word: Brief Reflections on the Sunday Readings*. Translated by Dennis D. Martin. San Francisco: Ignatius, 1983.

Balthasar, Hans Urs von. *My Work: In Retrospect*. San Francisco: Ignatius, 1993.

Balthasar, Hans Urs von. *Prayer*. Translated by Graham Harrison. San Francisco: Ignatius, 1986.

Balthasar, Hans Urs von. *A Short Primer for Unsettled Laymen*. Translated by Sister Mary Theresilde Skerry. San Francisco: Ignatius, 1985.

Balthasar, Hans Urs von. *Theo-Drama: Theological Dramatic Theory*. Vol. 2, *The Dramatis Personae: Man in God*, translated by Graham Harrison. San Francisco: Ignatius, 1990.

Balthasar, Hans Urs von. *Theo-Drama: Theological Dramatic Theory*. Vol. 4, *The Action*, translated by Graham Harrison. San Francisco: Ignatius, 1994.

Balthasar, Hans Urs von. *Theo-Drama: Theological Dramatic Theory*. Translated by Graham Harrison. Vol. 5, *The Last Act*. San Francisco: Ignatius, 1998.

Balthasar, Hans Urs von. *Theo-Logic: Theological Logical Theory*. Vol. 1, *Truth of the World*, translated by Adrian J. Walker. San Francisco: Ignatius, 2000.

Balthasar, Hans Urs von. *You Crown the Year with Your Goodness.* Translated by Graham Harrison. San Francisco: Ignatius, 1989.

Balthasar, Hans Urs von. *You Have Words of Eternal Life: Scripture Meditations.* Translated by Dennis Martin. San Francisco: Ignatius, 1991.

Balthasar, Hans Urs von, and Adrienne von Speyr. *To the Heart of the Mystery of Redemption.* Translated by Anne Englund Nash. San Francisco: Ignatius, 2010.

Bartlett, John. *Bartlett's Familiar Quotations.* Seventeenth edition. Edited by Justin Kaplan. Boston: Little, Brown and Company, 2002.

Benedict XVI. *God Is Love: Deus Caritas Est.* San Francisco: Ignatius, 2006.

Benedict XVI. *Jesus of Nazareth: From the Baptism in the Jordan to the Transfiguration.* New York: Doubleday, 2007.

Bernanos, Georges. *The Diary of a Country Priest.* Translated by Pamela Morris. New York: Doubleday, 1974.

Catechism of the Catholic Church. 2nd edition. Vatican City: Libreria Editrice Vaticana, 1997.

Crick, Francis. *The Astonishing Hypothesis: The Scientific Search for the Soul.* London: Simon & Schuster, 1994.

Dostoevsky, Fyodor. *The Brothers Karamazov.* Translated by Richard Pevear and Larissa Volokhonsky. San Francisco: North Point Press, 1990.

The Ignatius Catholic Study Bible: New Testament. Revised Standard Version. Second Catholic Edition. San Francisco: Ignatius Press, 2010.

John Paul II. *Ecclesia de Eucharistia.* Encyclical letter, April 17, 2003.

John Paul II. *Man and Woman He Created Them: A Theology of the Body.* Translated by Michael Waldstein. Boston: Pauline Books & Media, 2006.

Khema, Ayya and Zoketsu Norman Fischer. *Being Nobody, Going Nowhere: Meditations on the Buddhist Path.* Somerville, MA: Wisdom Publications, 2016.

Lewis, C. S. *The Four Loves.* New York: HarperCollins, 2017.

Lewis, C. S. *The Weight of Glory and Other Addresses.* San Francisco: HarperCollins, 2001.

Metzinger, Thomas. *Being No One: The Self-Model Theory of Subjectivity.* Cambridge, MA: Bradford Books, 2004.

Milton, John. *Paradise Lost.* New York: Heritage Press, 1940.

The Monotones. *(Who Wrote) The Book of Love.* Music and lyrics by Warren Davis, George Malone, and Charles Patrick. Chicago: Argo Records, 1957.

Montaigne, Michel de. *The Complete Essays of Montaigne.* Translated by Donald M. Frame. Stanford, CA: Stanford University Press, 2002.

The New Oxford American Dictionary, 2nd ed. Oxford, UK: Oxford University Press, 2005.

Pearce, Joseph. *Literature: What Every Catholic Should Know.* San Francisco: Ignatius Press, 2019.

Pieper, Josef. *Faith, Hope, Love.* San Francisco: Ignatius, 1997.

Plato. *Phaedrus, Ion, Gorgias, and Symposium, with Passages from The Republic and Laws,* translated by Lane Cooper. London: Oxford University Press, 1938.

Ratzinger, Joseph. *Behold the Pierced One.* San Francisco: Ignatius Press, 1986.

Ratzinger, Joseph. *Introduction to Christianity.* Revised edition. Translated by J. R. Foster. San Francisco: Ignatius Press, 2004.

Sartre, Jean-Paul. *No Exit and Three Other Plays.* New York: Vintage International, 1989.

Webster, Noah. *Webster's New Twentieth Century Dictionary: Unabridged.* Second edition. Edited by Jean L. McKechnie. New York: William Collins-World Publishers, 1979.

Winokur, Jon, ed. *Zen to Go,* New York: Penguin, 1990.

NOTES

¹ Originally recorded by The Monotones. Music and lyrics by Warren Davis, George Malone, and Charles Patrick.

² Pearce, *Literature: What Every Catholic Should Know*, 1.

³ Balthasar, *Heart of the World*, 203.

⁴ Ibid., 144.

⁵ Balthasar, *Explorations in Theology*. Vol. 5, *Man Is Created*, 172.

⁶ I am indebted to the theology of Hans Urs von Balthasar for many of these ideas.

⁷ Balthasar, *Prayer,* 207.

⁸ Balthasar, *Heart of the World*, 212.

⁹ Quoted in Jon Winokur, ed., *Zen to Go*, 64.

¹⁰ Balthasar, *Heart of the World*, 26-27.

¹¹ Ibid., 25.

¹² John Paul II, *Ecclesia de Eucharistia.*

¹³ https://www.pewresearch.org/fact-tank/2019/08/05/ transubstantiation-eucharist-u-s-catholics/

14 https://www.pewforum.org/religious-landscape-study/ at-tendance-at-religious-services/

15   https://earlychurchtexts.com/public/augustine_sermon_272_eucharist.htm

16 Pieper, *Faith, Hope, Love*, 164.

17 Lewis, *The Weight of Glory and Other Addresses*, 46.

18 Balthasar, *Heart of the World*, 94.

19 Balthasar, *Prayer*, 127-28.

20 Webster, *Webster's New Twentieth Century Dictionary: Un-abridged*, 1593.

21 Sartre, *No Exit*, 45.

22 Balthasar, *Explorations in Theology*. Vol. 5, *Man Is Created*, 65.

23 Ibid., 415.

24 Balthasar, *Explorations in Theology*. Vol. 4, *Spirit and Insti-tution*, 430.

25 Balthasar, *Theo-Drama: Theological Dramatic Theory*. Vol. 5, *The Last Act*, 105.

26 Balthasar, "The Fathers, the Scholastics, and Ourselves", 355.

27 Milton, *Paradise Lost*, bk. IV, line 73.

28 Compare "[Hell] is the suffering of being unable to love." Fyodor Dostoevsky, *The Brothers Karamazov*; and "'Hell, Mad-ame, is to love no longer.'" Georges Bernanos, *The Diary of a Country Priest*.

29 Ratzinger, *Introduction to Christianity*, 266.

[30] Balthasar, *Elucidations*, 254.

[31] *Catechism of the Catholic Church*, §§2006-2011.

[32] Balthasar, *In the Fullness of Faith*, 69.

[33] Balthasar, *Heart of the World*, 54.

[34] *The New Oxford American Dictionary*, 2nd ed., s.v. "ecstasy."

[35] Balthasar, *The Christian State of Life*, 75.

[36] *Introduction to Christianity*, 240.

[37] Balthasar, *You Have Words of Eternal Life: Scripture Meditations*, 89.

[38] Balthasar, *Elucidations*, 94.

[39] Balthasar, *Credo*, 101-02.

[40] *Essays*, I, 20. Cited in John Bartlett, *Bartlett's Familiar Quotations*, 152.

[41] Balthasar, *A Short Primer for Unsettled Laymen*, 101.

[42] *Prayer*, 128.

[43] Balthasar, *Light of the Word*, 312.

[44] Balthasar, *You Crown the Year with Your Goodness*, 214.

[45] Balthasar, *Theo-Drama: Theological Dramatic Theory*. Vol. 4, *The Action*, 331. Balthasar bases these ideas partly on the work of Sergei Bulgakov, the Russian Orthodox theologian.

[46] Balthasar, *The Christian State of Life*, 161.

[47] My portrayal of Jesus Christ as the open heart of God and the open heart of the world is based on Hans Urs von Balthasar's beautiful book, *Heart of the World*, which he described as a "hymn to Christ".

[48] The Virgin Mary is a special exception, preserved by God from sin for the sake of her unique mission as the Mother of God. *Catechism of the Catholic Church*, §§490-93.

[49] Brother Toby Lees, OP, "*Non nisi Te, Domine*", https://www.english.op.org/torch/17OT.

[50] Balthasar, addressing Jesus Christ: "[Y]our Heart is restless until it rests in me. Your Heart is restless until we rest in you, once time and eternity have become interfused." *Heart of the World*, 219.

[51] However, we *can* of course exert some conscious control over those feelings after they arise; we can choose to respond in ways that either increase or decrease the strength of those feelings; we can try to ignore or suppress the feelings, etc.

[52] Lewis, *The Four Loves*, 3.

[53] Saint Augustine: "If you do not know how to love yourself, you cannot truthfully love your neighbor." *Sermo* 368, 5; PL 39:1655. Cited in Pieper, *Faith, Hope, Love*, 237.

[54] A paraphrase of Thomas Aquinas' observation that we cannot *not* desire to be happy.

[55] Balthasar, *Theo-Drama: Theological Dramatic Theory*. Vol. 2, *The Dramatis Personae: Man in God*, 366.

[56] Pope Benedict XVI, *God Is Love: Deus Caritas Est*, §10.

[57] Plato, *Phaedrus*.

[58] Pieper, *Faith, Hope, Love*, 268. Several of the ideas contained in this meditation were drawn from Pieper's insightful discussion of sex on pages 246-71.

[59] John Paul II, *Man and Woman He Created Them: A Theology of the Body.*

[60] Pieper, *Faith, Hope, Love,* 273.

[61] Pieper, *Faith, Hope, Love,* 229.

[62] Lewis, *The Four Loves,* 73-74.

[63] Lewis, *The Four Loves,* 78, 83, 84.

[64]   https://www.land.com/lifestyle/off-grid-living-survival-guide/

[65] Balthasar, *The Glory of the Lord: A Theological Aesthetics.* Vol. 7, *Theology: The New Covenant,* 441.

[66] Balthasar, *Prayer,* 215.

[67] Compare *Catechism of the Catholic Church,* §§774, 1131.

[68] Balthasar, *Prayer,* 215; Balthasar, *Explorations in Theology.* Vol. 5, *Man Is Created,* 445.

[69] Pieper, *Faith, Hope, Love,* 202.

[70] Ibid., 202-03.

[71] *Catechism of the Catholic Church,* 882.

[72]   Bishop Robert Barron, "Hugging Anger", https://wordonfire.org/resources/homily/hugging-anger/28467/

[73] *Catechism of the Catholic Church,* §2546.

[74] *De diligendo Deo,* cited in Pieper, *Faith, Hope, Love,* 244.

[75] Pieper, *Faith, Hope, Love,* 244.

[76] This saying comes from a song entitled "The Best Things in Life Are Free," written by Buddy DeSylva and Lew Brown (lyrics) and Ray Henderson (music) for a 1927 musical entitled *Good*

News. The lyrics include the lines: "And love can come to everyone, The best things in life are free."

[77] Thomas Aquinas, *Summa contra Gentiles,* vol. 3, 26.

[78] Joseph Cardinal Ratzinger, *Behold the Pierced One,* 33-35.

[79] Balthasar, *Heart of the World,* 203.

[80] Consider, for example, the revealing contrast between the self-chosen moniker of the pro-abortion movement ("pro-*choice*") and that of the anti-abortion movement ("pro-*life*"). In the pro-abortion movement, the power to "choose" is elevated above life itself.

[81] Balthasar, *Theo-Drama: Theological Dramatic Theory.* Vol. 2, *The Dramatis Personae: Man in God,* 233.

[82] Balthasar, *The Christian State of Life,* 72.

[83] Saint Augustine, *Confessions,* 1, 1, 1.

[84] *The Ignatius Catholic Study Bible: New Testament,* 369.

[85] "We who are trying to follow [Jesus], we will work with all our power to promote the Kingdom of God, justice between men, but first of all by changing the dispositions of hearts, by opening them to those of the Heart of Jesus...." Balthasar, *To the Heart of the Mystery of Redemption,* 60-61. See also Balthasar, *You Crown the Year with Your Goodness,* 25, 255.

[86] Several of these ideas in this reflection are drawn from the theology of Hans Urs von Balthasar, who has emphasized the importance of a renewed focus on beauty in theology and in our culture at large. See, for example, *The Glory of the Lord: A Theological Aesthetics.* Vol. 1, *Seeing the Form,* 115-16 and 592; *The Glory of*

the Lord: A Theological Aesthetics. Vol. 2, Studies in Theological Style: Clerical Styles, 11; The Glory of the Lord: A Theological Aesthetics. Vol. 4, The Realm of Metaphysics in Antiquity, 391; The Glory of the Lord: A Theological Aesthetics. Vol. 5, The Realm of Metaphysics in the Modern Age, 253; and Theo-Drama: Theological Dramatic Theory. Vol. 2, The Dramatis Personae: Man in God, 88.

[87] Cited by Balthasar in The Glory of the Lord: A Theological Aesthetics. Vol. 5, The Realm of Metaphysics in the Modern Age, 190.

[88] Lewis, The Weight of Glory, 42.

[89] Balthasar, The Glory of the Lord: A Theological Aesthetics. Vol. 1, Seeing the Form, 18.

[90] Balthasar, Theo-Logic: Theological Logical Theory. Vol. 1, Truth of the World, 9.

[91] Balthasar, My Work: In Retrospect, 116.

[92] Saint Bonaventure.

[93] Pope Benedict XVI, Jesus of Nazareth: From the Baptism in the Jordan to the Transfiguration, 268.

[94] Balthasar, Theo-Logic: Theological Logical Theory. Vol. 1, Truth of the World, 37.

[95] Balthasar, Explorations in Theology. Vol. 5, Man Is Created, 327.

[96] Balthasar, Light of the Word, 90.

[97] Ayya Khema and Zoketsu Norman Fischer.

---

⁹⁸ Recorded by a band named "Starf*cker" and released by Polyvinyl Record Co. in 2016.

⁹⁹ Metzinger, *Being No One: The Self-Model Theory of Subjectivity.*

¹⁰⁰ Crick, *The Astonishing Hypothesis: The Scientific Search for the Soul,* 3.

¹⁰¹ Compare the famous line from the opera entitled *The Gondoliers* by Sir William Schwenck Gilbert, the lyricist half of Gilbert and Sullivan: "When everyone is somebodee, then no one's anybody!" There's also a similar line from the film entitled *The Incredibles,* written by Brad Bird, produced by Pixar Animation Studios, and released by Walt Disney Pictures in 2004: "[W]hen everyone's super, no one will be...."